Advance Praise for Intertwingled

"Intertwingled is a meditation on the connectedness of everything. From language and ontology to culture and strategy, Peter takes us on a journey that reveals how a simple change in what we take for granted can send ripples that reach far beyond our awareness."

Irene Au, Operating Partner, Khosla Ventures

"In the information age, we are all information architects, says Morville in this fresh and fascinating take on the discipline he played a huge part in creating. Drawing on nature, culture, history, and science, plus decades of deep personal experience helping major clients, Morville finds new and profound meaning in the business of helping users to find their way."

Jeffrey Zeldman, author, Designing with Web Standards

"MIND BLOWN OPEN, rearranged, and reshaped. This startling book took me on a twisty adventure in how to think, see, design, and experience the world differently. It's like stepping through a door to a shifted universe that's richer, deeper, more connected. And, Peter reveals practical ideas and insights about how to build understanding and cope with complexity. Say goodbye to your current self when you start this book, because you won't be the same person by the end of the journey."

Kathy Sierra, author, Badass: Making Users Awesome

"If James Burke, Donella Meadows, John Berger, and Peter Morville had dinner together on a quiet Friday evening, this book would be the record of their conversation. Just as much a spirited look at systems design, as it is a way of looking at the world. Essential."

Liz Danzico, Creative Director, NPR

"How does Peter Morville manage all the suffering and turbulence in modern information architecture? Having read this book, I now know. The guy has become a guru. He's achieved enlightenment."

Bruce Sterling, author, Shaping Things, co-founder, EFF

"This is a delightful, surprisingly practical book: an insider's guide to the best thinking on design, culture, and complex systems. True to his vocation, Morville makes it easy to find useful tidbits, while also opening doors and illuminating connections. Shining through it all is an invitation to expand our notion of what information architecture entails – and what it really takes to change the world. *Intertwingled* is a fine dinner party of a book, and Morville is a marvelous host."

Vienna Teng, singer, songwriter, pianist

"*Intertwingled* is exactly the book you'd expect from a volume with that fanciful title. Delightful. Full of unexpected connections. Panoramic. Practical. Wise. Anyone who makes the case that the Buddha was an information architect, as Peter Morville artfully does, is worth your attention. You won't find a better guide to surviving and succeeding in a world of hyper-abundant information."

Lee Rainie, Director, Pew Research Center's Internet Project

"Intermingles great thinking about interaction design with deep dives into spiritual, physical, and personal dimensions. Morville's generosity with his own stories enriches a work of great insight on a topic that is ironically not seen as personal. From systems thinking to culture and politics, this work is deeply and diversely informed. *Intertwingled* is required reading for cultural interventionists."

Brenda Laurel, author, Computers as Theatre

"Peter Morville gently leads us to a place we can be still in discomfort. The book appears to be about information architecture, but the true value of this narrative is its appeal to a general audience. Readers outside the industry will identify themselves in Morville's story. It will guide them into a better understanding of their relationship to information and perhaps incidentally into their own public library."

Josie Barnes Parker, Director, Ann Arbor District Library

"*Intertwingled* offers its reader a beautiful, personal journey into connectedness, a gentle invitation to reflect upon the nature of change, and a refreshingly honest exploration of life in a complex world."

Dave Gray, author, The Connected Company

Intertwingled

PETER MORVILLE

To Mike,
Thanks for making me a part
of the Digital Strategy Summit!
Peter Morville

SEMANTIC STUDIOS
ANN ARBOR, MICHIGAN

Intertwingled: Information Changes Everything

by Peter Morville

Semantic Studios

109 Catherine Street

Ann Arbor, Michigan 48104

Web: semanticstudios.com

Email: morville@semanticstudios.com

Editor: Peter Morville

Cover Designers: Jeff Callender and Peter Morville

Interior Designers: Jeff Callender and Peter Morville

Illustrators: Peter Morville and Jeff Callender

ISBN: 978-0-692-22558-5

LCCN: 2014913166

Contents

Preface

*"People keep pretending they can make
things hierarchical, categorizable, and
sequential when they can't. Everything is
deeply intertwingled."*

– THEODOR HOLM NELSON

In 1974, Theodor H. Nelson wrote and self-published a book
with two covers. The first, *Computer Lib*, is an introduction to
computers that notes "any nitwit can understand computers,
and many do." The flip side, *Dream Machines*, is an invitation
to the future of media and cognition that states "everything is
deeply intertwingled." This prescient codex served as a bible
to many pioneers of the personal computer and the Internet.

In 1994, I started my career as an information architect. I was
driven by the belief that we can make the world a better place
by organizing its information. Together, Lou Rosenfeld and I
built a company and wrote a book that helped to establish the
field of information architecture. Ever since, I've been blessed

with opportunities to do what I love. But a few years ago, I began to sense a glitch. My ability to help my clients was limited by our narrow focus. This was partly my fault for defining myself as a specialist, but I eventually came to see that this problem of reductionism is endemic to our culture.

In 2014, I wrote this book to show Ted Nelson's insight that everything is deeply intertwingled is more vital than ever, and to argue we can *get better at getting better* by changing how we organize information, not only on websites, but in our minds. It was not an easy book to write, and if its reading makes you uncomfortable, then perhaps it has met my ambition.

Organization of This Book

This book should be read in linear style from start to end. It's divided into chapters, but of course they are all intertwingled.

Chapter 1, Nature

Explores the nature of information in systems from the wolves of Isle Royale to Uber in Silicon Valley. Explains why systems thinking is essential if we hope to create sustainable change.

Chapter 2, Categories

A deep dive into classification and its consequences. Flows from organizing for users to organizing ourselves (*governance*). Covers embodied cognition, meditation, and moral circles.

Chapter 3, Connections

The history of links from hypertext and navigation to planning and prediction. Explores self-justification and the cobra effect. Blames music and synesthesia on the architecture of the brain.

Chapter 4, Culture

Offers models for understanding and changing organizational and national culture. Covers ways of knowing from authority to intuition and ways of changing from tiny habits to positive deviance. Features a thick description of design ethnography.

Chapter 5, Limits

A journey beyond the limits of understanding and growth that includes iatrogenics, teleportation, and meatballs. Tackles big fish from pollution and corruption to extinction and collapse. Explains why our myths are the root cause and our only hope.

Acknowledgments

Abby Covert, Andrew Hinton, Christian Crumlish, Richard Dalton, and Noriyo Asano read the manuscript and provided generous advice and support. Jeffery Callender and I worked together to design the cover, interior layout, and illustrations. The symbols and icons are licensed from The Noun Project. Andrea Resmini, Bob Royce, Chris Farnum, Christina Wodtke, Dan Cooney, Dan Klyn, Dave Gray, David Fiorito, Whitney Hess, Heidi Weise, Jane Dysart, Jason Hobbs, Jorge Arango, Joseph Janes, Livia Labate, Louis Rosenfeld, Peter Merholz, Thomas Wendt, and Simon St. Laurent, and are a few of the folks who inspired and helped me along the way. Last but not least, I'd like to thank Malcolm, Judith, Paul, and Ros for being in my circle; Susan, Claire, and Claudia for *intertwingling* my life with love; and Knowsy for our long evening walks.

Nature

"When we try to pick out anything by itself, we find it hitched to everything else in the universe."

– JOHN MUIR

I'm standing on an island beach in the northwest corner of Lake Superior. After nine hours in my Honda Civic and six hours aboard the Ranger III, my backpack and I have been transported into the wilderness archipelago of *Isle Royale National Park*. While this rugged, isolated refuge is among the least visited of our national parks, it's well-known among ecologists for its wolf and moose, subjects of the longest continuous study of a predator-prey relationship in the world.

Of course, I'm not here as a scientist. I'm here to hike. But I was drawn to this place by the story of its ecosystem. When the study began in 1958, well-established mathematical models of predation described how the populations should rise and fall as part of a cyclical, co-evolutionary pattern that maintains the "balance of nature." For the first few years, things proceeded as expected. But the ecologist, Durward Allen, had the foresight to persevere beyond the normal period of observation, and the dramatic, dynamic variation that unfolded was an illuminating surprise.

> The more we studied, the more we came to realize how poor our previous explanations had been. The accuracy of our predictions for Isle Royale wolf and moose populations is comparable to those for long-term weather and financial markets. Every five-year period in the Isle Royale history has been different from every other five-year period – even after fifty years of close observation.[1]

This is a lesson in humility, and a sign of what's to come for those who labor in today's high-tech ecologies. In user experience and digital strategy, there's a lot of talk about "ecosystems" that integrate devices and touchpoints across channels. While this is a step in the right direction, our models and prescriptions belie the true complexity of our information systems and the organizations they are designed to serve.

Recently, while I was consulting with a Fortune 500 that does over $2 billion a year in online sales, one of my clients explained that over the years he'd seen lots of consultants fail to create lasting change. "They tell us to improve consistency, so we clean up our website, but the clutter soon comes back. We keep making the same mistakes, over and over."

This infinite loop to nowhere results from treating symptoms without knowing the cause, a bad habit with which we're all too familiar. Part of our problem is human nature. We're impatient. We choose immediate gratification and the illusion of efficiency over the longer, harder but more effective course of action. And part of our problem is culture. Our institutions and mindsets remain stuck in the industrial age. Businesses are designed as machines, staffed by specialists in silos. Each person does their part, but nobody understands the whole.

The machine view was so successful during the industrial revolution, we find it astonishingly hard to let go, even as the information age renders it obsolete and counterproductive in a growing set of contexts. It's not that the old model is all wrong. We're not about to throw away hierarchy or specialization. But our world is changing, and we must adjust.

The information age amplifies *connectedness*. Each wave of change – web, social, mobile, the Internet of Things – increases the degree and import of connection and accelerates the rate of change. In this context, it's vital to see our organizations as ecosystems. This is not meant figuratively. Our organizations are ecosystems, literally. And while each community of organisms plus environment may function as a unit, the web of connections and consequences extends beyond its borders.

All ecosystems are linked. To understand any complex, adaptive system, we must look outside its limits. For instance, the story of Isle Royale is a lesson in systems thinking. In 1958, predictions for the rise and fall of populations were grounded in classic predation theory: more moose, more wolves, but more wolves, less moose, and less moose, less wolves, and so on. It's an interesting, useful model, but it's incomplete.

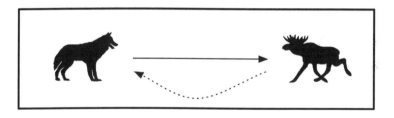

Figure 1-1. The classic predator-prey relationship.

By 1969 the number of moose had doubled, a major shift in balance. By 1980 the moose population had tripled, then declined by half, and the number of wolves had doubled. Ecologists wondered whether the wolves might drive their prey to extinction. But two years later, the wolf population had been decimated by canine parvovirus, a disease that was accidentally introduced by a visitor who (illegally) brought his dog to the island.

Over the years, the moose population has grown steadily only to collapse due to cold winters, hot summers, and outbreaks of moose tick. The tiny wolf population failed to thrive for years due to inbreeding. But in the winter of 1997, a lone male wolf crossed an ice bridge between Isle Royale and Canada, and revitalized the population for a while. Today, however, the wolves are again at risk of extinction, and scientists fear that due to global warming, no more ice bridges will form.[2]

What's interesting for our purposes is that the surprises in this story result from *exogenous shocks*. They come from outside the model of the system. In ecology and economics, such disruptions are often explained away as rare, unpredictable, and unworthy of further study. But that's an ignorant, dangerous conclusion. The truth is that the model is wrong.

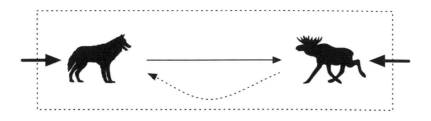

Figure 1-2. Systems are subject to exogenous shocks.

We make this mistake over and over in the systems we build. We work on websites as if they exist in a vacuum. We forge ahead without mapping the ecosystems of users and content creators. We measure success and reward performance without knowing how governance and culture impact individuals and teams. We plan, code, and design wearing blinders, then act surprised when we're blindsided by change.

If we hope to understand and manage a complex, dynamic system, we must practice the art of *frame shifting*. When our focus is narrow, our ability to predict or shape outcomes is nil. So we must learn to see our systems anew by soliciting divergent views. And when we uncover hidden connections, information flows, and feedback loops that transgress the borders of our mental model, we must change the model.

In the era of ecosystems, seeing the big picture is more important than ever, and less likely. It's not simply that we're forced into little boxes by organizational silos and professional specialization. We like it in there. We feel safe. But we're not. This is no time to stick to your knitting. We must go from boxes to arrows. Tomorrow belongs to those who connect.

If this talk of change disturbs you, that's good. Learning makes us all uncomfortable. When faced with disruption, we're tempted to turn back. But if we press on, we build skills and understanding that may prove invaluable to us in the future. Once we overcome our initial fear and discomfort, we may even begin to enjoy ourselves. Some of life's best paths start out on slippery rocks. Or at least that's what I tell myself as I stand on the beach of Isle Royale, with my backpack, map and compass, anxiously gnawing on a hunk of meatless jerky.

It's not that I'm afraid of the wolves. There aren't many left. I'm worried because I've never been backpacking. My hikes always end in hotels. The last time I slept in a tent was at Foo Camp, a hacker event during which attendees camp in an apple orchard behind the offices of O'Reilly Media. And I couldn't sleep. I was cold. My hips hurt. That morning, shivering in my tent but grateful for the orchard Wi-Fi, I fired up my Apple MacBook Pro and booked a hotel. But now, I'm headed into the wilderness alone, for four days and four nights. I'm 44 years old, and this is my first time.

Of course, it's my own fault. Since turning 40, I've been making myself uncomfortable on purpose. At an age when it's easy to fall into a rut, I've run my first marathon, tried the triathlon, and tackled new consulting challenges that terrified me. Now, I'm writing and publishing a book, and carrying a bed on my back. And I invite you to join me in discomfort. Because it's not just my age. It's our age. It's the information age, a time when learning how to learn (and unlearn) is central to success. Instead of hiding from change, let's embrace it. Each time we try something new, we get better at getting better. Experience builds competence and confidence, so we're ready for the big changes, like re-thinking what we do.

Information in Systems

When I graduated from college in 1991, I had no plan, so I moved in with my parents. I worked by day (*mind-numbing data entry*) and messed around on my computer at night. One Saturday, while browsing the public library, I stumbled upon a tattered old book about careers in library science. As I learned about libraries, I thought about the networks – AOL, CompuServe, Prodigy – I'd been exploring. They were a mess. It was hard to find things. Could librarianship be practiced in these online computer networks? That question sent me to graduate school at the University of Michigan.

In 1992, I started classes at the School of Information and Library Studies, and promptly began to panic. I was stuck in required courses like Reference and Cataloging with people who wanted to be librarians. In hindsight, I'm glad I took those classes, but at the time I was convinced I'd made a very big mistake. It took a while to find my groove. I studied information retrieval and database design. I explored Dialog, the world's first commercial online search service. And I fell madly in love with the Internet.

The tools were crude, the content sparse, but the promise irresistible. A global network of networks that provides universal access to ideas and information: how could anyone who loves knowledge resist that? I was hooked. I dedicated myself to "the design of information systems."

Thus, when I left library school, I knew what I wanted to do. But there were no jobs. So I became an entrepreneur, working with Lou Rosenfeld and Joseph Janes to grow *Argus Associates*. We taught people how to use the Internet, we built networked, hierarchical, text-only information systems using the Gopher protocol. And when Mosaic, the first graphical browser (*pretty pictures but no back button*), was released, we began doing what folks today would recognize as website design.

We dabbled in everything from coding to content, but specialized in helping our clients to structure and organize websites. There wasn't a name for this work, so we called it "information architecture" and set out to establish a new field of practice. At first we relied heavily on the metaphor. We talked about architectural plans and blueprints and invoked wayfinding and the familiar frustration of getting lost.

In time our explanations grew more concrete. We focused on the organization, labeling, search, and navigation systems of websites that help users complete tasks, find what they need, and understand what they find. In the late 90s, this concentration made sense. Everyone was shoveling content onto their sites, and somebody needed to organize it.

Our formal definition of information architecture as "the structural design of shared information environments" was more expansive, but nobody remembers definitions. What caught people's attention were the wireframes, the most visible yet superficial element of our work. So, in the minds of many, our practice was wedded to websites and wireframes.

But, as we shifted from nineties to noughties, information architecture continued to evolve. In addition to wireframes, we used all sorts of tools and methods to learn about users, test ideas, and make the complex clear. And, we went beyond usability, working hard to improve findability, accessibility, credibility, and other qualities of the user experience.

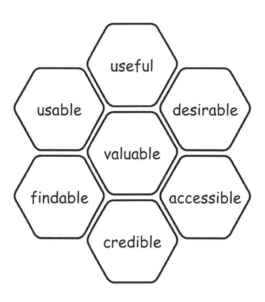

Figure 1-3. The User Experience Honeycomb.

Along the way, the context in which we practice changed. Web search and SEO turned sites upside down, by shifting attention from home pages to the design of findable, social objects that serve as both destination and gateway. In short, we began to plan for multiple front doors.

We embraced Web 2.0 selectively, learning to design rules, frameworks, and architectures of participation. And we started making maps for mobile and cross-channel services and experiences to help our clients and colleagues to see and understand what's possible and desirable.

We realized that, in the modern era of cross-channel experiences and product-service systems, it makes less and less sense to design taxonomies, sitemaps, and wireframes without also mapping the customer journey, modeling the system dynamics, and analyzing the impacts upon business processes, incentives, and the org chart.

As our practice evolved and the gap between classic and contemporary information architecture grew, our community struggled to explain itself, so much so we earned a hashtag (#dtdt) for "defining the damn thing." And while accusations of navel-gazing were not without merit, this was a necessary, productive struggle that helped us shed a web-centric worldview in favor of a medium-independent perspective.

Andrea Resmini and Luca Rosati led us to independence with their manifesto for pervasive information architecture.

> Information architectures become ecosystems. When different media and different contexts are tightly intertwined, no artifact can stand as a single isolated entity. Every single artifact becomes an element in a larger ecosystem.[3]

Soon they were joined by new voices. Jorge Arango, a traditional architect by training, put a new twist on the old metaphor by arguing that where architects use forms and spaces to design environments for inhabitation, information architects use nodes and links to create environments for understanding.[4] Andrew Hinton invited us to peer through the lens of embodied cognition to see that digital contexts are every bit as real as their physical counterparts and to see that language is environment and information is architecture.[5] And Dan Klyn inspired us to "make things be good" by learning from the lifework of Richard Saul Wurman and by focusing on the architecture part of IA.[6]

I'm excited by the depth and diversity of ideas about the direction of our discipline. And yet I worry we may be unbalanced. In our passion for placemaking we mustn't lose sight of the information in the architecture. Our strength in structural design must be joined by an aptitude for managing information flows, feedback loops, and motivational metrics.

What matters most isn't what we build but the change we make. That's why I'm writing this book. I want to study, understand, and clarify *the nature of information in systems*. In part, it's about going beyond the Web. Mobile and the Internet of Things are tearing down the walls between physical and digital, creating new information flows and loops.

It's also about seeing old sites with fresh eyes. Our websites aren't just channels for marketing and communication. They've become rich, dynamic places where work gets done. Websites are extensions of the organization that change its nature. To manage them, we must address inputs, outputs, feedback loops, metrics, governance, and culture.

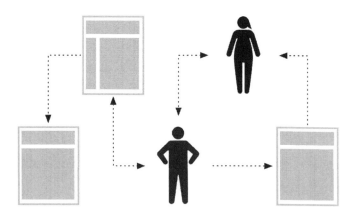

Figure 1-4. Websites are part of organizational ecosystems.

But that's not enough. We should set our sights higher. Life is too short to focus solely on getting better at business. Society as a whole suffers from bad decisions and anxiety caused by misinformation, disinformation, filter failure, and information illiteracy. We can't expect technology to save the day.

While the Internet has delivered great change to consumers and industries, it hasn't made as much progress in education, healthcare, and government. And we've begun to learn the cost of free. In recent years, we've begun to lose newspapers, bookstores, libraries, and privacy. Now we search for answers in a sea of advertisements, thinking carefully (or not) about where to look, who to trust, and what to believe.

These are wicked problems but not impossible. No field has all the answers, but together we can do better. That's why I'm writing outside my category about the nature of information in systems. It's not all about information architecture, and I'm a long way from library school. But this inquiry is important. Connectedness has consequences. Information changes everything. That's why I'm willing to travel.

Systems Thinking

I'm in Silicon Valley. I'm in a cab headed to my hotel. Actually, that's not true. I'm hitchhiking and plan to sleep with a stranger named Sophie. Okay, that's not quite right either. But that's how our eleven year old daughter explained my experiment with Uber and Airbnb to my wife.

Yes, once again, I'm making myself uncomfortable. I'm an advisor to the School of Library and Information Science at San José State University. Since 2009, the program has embraced a 100% online model. Ironically, I'm here for a face to face meeting. And I'm using this visit to California as an opportunity to dip my toes into the infamous *sharing economy*.

So, I'm not in a cab, and I'm not hitchhiking. I'm in a black town car with an Uber-qualified driver named Gustavo. I hailed him via mobile app. I must admit it was fun watching the little black car icon drive to my location. I already know a bit about my driver. He's passed Uber's insurance and background checks and has a 5 star rating. At the end of my flat rate ride (paid by phone) I can rate him and even write a review. Of course, while I'm rating Gustavo, he's also rating me, which matters because drivers often ignore the requests of customers with three stars or less. So, if I'm obnoxious or give him a bad rating, he may return the favor, and cost me a ride. The system isn't perfect, but neither are taxis.

We've all struggled to hail a cab or waited in line or on hold. And we've all endured rudeness, bad driving, and cabbies who simply get lost. But not all of us suffer alike. While in Washington, D.C. a few years ago, I helped a friend catch a cab. A taxi pulled over, but when the driver saw my friend would be riding alone, he drove away before she could get in. I was shocked, but she wasn't. As a black woman, she'd been there before. This bigotry is nearly invisible in the world of yellow cabs, but it would be hard to hide in Uber. They've built a new "architecture of trust" that re-frames the rules and relationships between passengers and drivers.

The design of these information systems is tricky. Before pickup, Uber drivers and passengers see each other's ratings and may decline a ride based on the number of stars. After a ride, drivers see the rating they're given but not the review. Passengers see neither. Drivers are told by Uber not to solicit 5-star ratings, nor confront passengers about low ratings, but both do occur. Balancing privacy and transparency for optimal performance and trust in the system requires constant tuning.

Figure 1-5. Rideshares rely on trust and ratings.

Despite these challenges, Uber has built a platform that integrates mobile phones, social networks, and GPS to disrupt the business of transport. Their success is evident in the backlash from rage over "surge pricing" to lawsuits and fines in cities around the world. Interestingly, their defense is all about categorization. Uber insists they are not a taxi company nor a limo service. They simply match drivers and passengers. So they aren't subject to established regulations, licensing, or insurance requirements.

Uber isn't alone in this argument. They have competition. For instance, there's Lyft, a peer-to-peer rideshare whose drivers don't charge "fares" but receive "donations" from passengers who are encouraged to sit in the front seat and give the driver a fistbump. Their tagline is "your friend with a car." Do we need any more evidence that a Lyft is not a taxi?

Meanwhile, taxis aren't standing still. They're adopting e-hail apps that enable passengers to book regular taxis with their mobile device. In short, from lawsuits to competition, Uber has plenty of problems. This is to be expected. Disruptive innovation inevitably provokes a response.

Or, in the words of John Gall, "the system always kicks back." In *Systemantics*, a witty, irreverent book published in 1975, Gall uses the example of garbage collection to explain that when we create a system to accomplish a goal, a new entity comes into being: the system itself.

> After setting up a garbage-collection system, we find ourselves faced with a new universe of problems. These include questions of collective bargaining with the garbage collectors' union, rates and hours, collection on very cold or rainy days, purchase and maintenance of garbage trucks, millage and bond issues, voter apathy, regulations regarding the separation of garbage from trash…if the collectors bargain for more restrictive definitions of garbage, refusing to pick up twigs, trash, old lamps, and even leaving behind properly wrapped garbage if it is not placed within a regulation can, so that taxpayers resort to clandestine dumping along the highway, this exemplifies the Principle of Le Chatelier: the system tends to oppose its own proper function.[7]

This is why we need disruptive innovation within our society. Systems that have grown unresponsive must be shaken up. But, like garbage, change is messy. Disruptors such as Uber provoke counterattacks, and they build new systems that create new problems. All of this change results in unintended consequences that are hard to predict or control.

While we'll never be perfect at change, we can be better. One path to progress runs through the field of systems thinking, an approach that aims to understand how the parts relate to the whole. Think about it. We're all familiar with Aristotle's aphorism: "the whole is greater than the sum of its parts." But how often do we put this into practice? How often do we take time to understand the whole before doing our part?

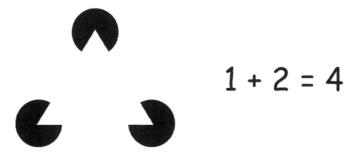

Figure 1-6. The whole is greater than the sum of its parts.

It's not easy. Our society is organized around the opposing principle that the whole equals the sum of the parts. Reductionism, the idea that any system can be understood by studying its parts, was introduced by the ancient Greeks and formalized by French philosopher René Descartes in the 17th century. During the ensuing scientific and industrial revolutions, reductionism and specialization were so spectacularly successful, they became embedded within our culture. In school, we divide knowledge into subjects and kids into grades. In business, we put specialists in silos and progress in quarters. Our categories are like water to a fish, so ubiquitous and "natural," we don't even know they're there.

Again, it's not that it's all wrong. Reductionism is truly valuable. In fact, its value is part of the problem. Success blinds us to alternatives. And, we're reaching its limits. Optimizing for efficiency through specialization eventually compromises overall effectiveness. Plus, some problems can't be solved as parts. Economic volatility, political corruption, crime, drug addiction, lifestyle disease, and environmental degradation are systemic. Nobody creates these problems on purpose or wants them to continue. They emerge from the system and are wholly immune to the quick fix.

That's where systems thinking comes in. While conventional thinking uses *analysis* to break things down, systems thinking relies on *synthesis* to see the whole and the interactions between parts. As Russell Ackoff, a pioneer in systems thinking and business management, explains:

> Systems thinking looks at relationships (rather than unrelated objects), connectedness, process (rather than structure), the whole (rather than just its parts), the patterns (rather than the contents) of a system, and context. Thinking systematically also requires several shifts in perception, which lead in turn to different ways to teach, and different ways to organize society.[8]

There's a subversive dimension to systems thinking with hints of danger and risk. And this talk of change can overwhelm. We can't have everyone thinking this way. But, at times, we need activists and entrepreneurs who can see the system as the source of its own problems, and restructure it. Progress depends upon people who know there must be a better way.

These change agents are often found in and around information systems, because our tools of communication are powerful levers of change. As the legendary systems thinker and environmentalist Donella Meadows explains:

> Some interconnections in systems are actual physical flows, such as the water in the tree's trunk or the students progressing through a university. Many interconnections are flows of information – signals that go to decision points or action points within a system…information holds systems together.[9]

In her book, *Thinking in Systems*, Donella makes it clear most problems in systems are due to biased, late, or missing information; and adding or restoring information is often the most powerful intervention. Simply changing the length of a delay may radically change behavior, causing overshoots, oscillations, and even total collapse of the system. Feedback loops are central to the design of information in systems.

Donella tells a great story about electric meters in Dutch houses. In the 1970s, a subdivision was built near Amsterdam with houses that were identical except for the position of the electric meter. Some were in the basement while others were in the front hall. Over time, the houses with visible meters (in the front hall) consumed thirty percent less electricity. She describes this as "an example of a high leverage point in the information structure of the system. It's not a parameter adjustment, not a strengthening or weakening of an existing feedback loop. It's a new loop delivering feedback to a place where it wasn't going before."[10]

This is where information architects can make a difference. Our user research and stakeholder interviews illuminate the openings where what's desirable meets what's possible. And we're already in the business of mapping interconnections and information flows. If we take the time to understand the nature of information in systems, we can shape profound change with the right mix of links, loops, and levers.

Of course, it's not enough for us to understand. We must also convince our clients and colleagues. As information architects, we've learned to reveal the infrastructure behind the interface. We're experts at using boxes and arrows to make the invisible visible. This need for visualization is something we share with systems thinkers like Donella, who explains:

> There is a problem in discussing systems only with words. Words and sentences must, by necessity, come only one at a time in linear, logical order. Systems happen all at once. They are connected not just in one direction, but in many directions simultaneously. To discuss them properly, it is necessary to use a language that shares some of the same properties as the phenomena under discussion.[11]

Both practices rely upon a visual language for analysis and design. While information architects are known for our sitemaps and wireframes, the tool of choice for systems thinkers is the stock-and-flow diagram.

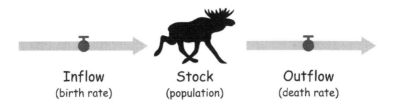

Figure 1-7. A simple stock-and-flow.

The simplest use only stocks (*elements*) and flows (*in and out*), while complex models integrate the feedback loops, limits, and delays that produce growth, self-organization, hierarchy, oscillation, dynamic equilibrium, resilience, and collapse. This simple language can describe the most complex phenomena.

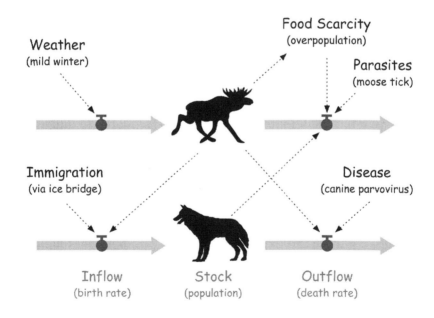

Figure 1-8. A more complex stock and flow.

Of course, the more complex the diagram, the harder it is to understand. The process of making a map helps us rise above the limits of the local to see the whole, but this bird's-eye view isn't suitable for all audiences. Often we must aim for simple visuals that make the complex clear, focus attention, and transform ideas and understanding into decisive action.

Either way, we mustn't limit our practice to boxes and arrows. There are myriad ways to visualize systems and their possibilities. Donella may overstate her case, for even when words come one at a time, the narrative that emerges is often nonlinear. Good stories tend to wander. They draw upon our memories, associations, and emotions to create rich, sensory experience. Often, words are the best way to paint a picture.

In *The Death and Life of Great American Cities*, Jane Jacobs does this brilliantly. In a text with no image, she helps us see the city as a system. Her words bring sidewalks, parks, and neighborhoods to life. Jane shows us why traditional maps aren't good for urban planning. By focusing on roads and buildings, maps reveal the skeleton but miss the point. A city's structure is evident in its mixture of uses, the life and activity it nurtures, and the conditions that generate diversity. To see and improve our cities, we must use a different lens.

> Imagine a large field in darkness. In the field, many fires are burning. They are of many sizes, some great, others small; some far apart, others dotted close together; some are brightening, some are slowly going out. Each fire, large or small, extends its radiance into the surrounding murk, and thus it carves out a space. But the space and the shape of that space exist only to the extent that the light from the fire creates it. The murk has no shape or pattern except where it is carved into space by the light. When the murk between the lights becomes deep and undefinable and shapeless, the only way to give it form or structure is to kindle new fires in the murk or sufficiently enlarge the nearest existing fires.[12]

We've all felt the warmth and vitality of populous city streets, and we've also felt fear in the cold, dark, lost areas. Jane's words help us see why this picture, rather than a classic map, is the right frame for city planning. It's an unconventional text that explains why slums stay slums and traffic gets worse. So it's no surprise that Jane Jacobs was a systems thinker.

> To see complex systems of functional order as order, and not as chaos, takes understanding. The leaves dropping from the trees in autumn, the interior of an airplane engine, the entrails of a dissected rabbit, the city desk of a newspaper, all appear to be chaos if they are seen without comprehension. Once they are understood as systems of order, they actually *look* different.[13]

Her 1961 book was an attack on conventional city planning and a perfect illustration of systems thinking. Jane recognized cities as problems in organized complexity, a jumble of parts interrelated into an organic whole. She believed good cities foster social interaction at the street level. They support walking, biking, and public transit over cars. They get people talking to each other. Residential buildings have porches. Sidewalks and parks have benches. Safe neighborhoods are mixed-use with "eyes on the street" all day. Jane's vision was hopeful, and she made an impact. Her text is required reading in urban studies. Her ideas have become conventional wisdom. Our world is more livable because of her.

Sadly, not all cities got the message. As my black Uber car cruises the freeways of San José, I'm besieged by the image of urban sprawl. It's hard to feel at home in a place like this. But it's not just the office parks and strip malls that are making me uncomfortable. I'm worried about meeting Sophie. Part of the reason I don't participate in the sharing economy is I'm an introvert, and a shy one too. Hotels are easy. Staff rarely say more than hello. But Airbnb is different. I'm staying in a home with my host. It's like crashing with a friend you don't know.

Of course, Sophie comes highly recommended. She has a 5-star rating and dozens of glowing reviews. I'm not at all worried about safety or security. And while I'm not sure I'd want our daughters being Airbnb hosts, I'm not a complete stranger to Sophie. She's seen my profile, references, and Facebook account. She knows I have a verified ID. Airbnb has my home address, phone number, credit card, and driver's license. I'm about as far from anonymity as can be. And her property is protected by a one million dollar host guarantee. Airbnb has invested in an architecture of trust that helps them scale up safely to serve millions of guests around the world.

Figure 1-9. Airbnb's architecture of trust.

But like Uber they do have problems. In New York, Airbnb has been declared illegal, and landlords given big fines. In Paris, hosts unwittingly rented to prostitutes who used their home as a brothel. All around the world, neighbors are disturbed by the presence of strangers in what they thought were single-family homes. And, of course, hotels are furious. They're losing business. So they insist on enforcing the laws.

All innovations have unintended consequences, and the system always kicks back. These are lessons we must heed as we take information to the next level. Mobile apps aren't products. They are service avatars that link users into business ecosystems. Websites aren't products either. They are systems within systems. That's why content management is messier than garbage collection, and why information architects must be systems thinkers. When strategy and structure meet people and process, our maps must be subject to change, because things rarely go according to plan.

Intervention

In recent years, I've had the honor and privilege of working with the Library of Congress, our nation's oldest cultural institution. As a library school graduate, an opportunity to advise the world's largest library is about as good as it gets. But our relationship got off to a rocky start.

I was invited to evaluate the Library's web presence. So I conducted a holistic study that included user research, stakeholder interviews, and expert review. I learned that the Library had over 100 websites, many with unique domain names, identities, and navigation systems. And most users had absolutely no idea which site to visit for which purpose.

I wrote up a brutally honest report. I compared the Library's fragmented web presence to the Winchester Mystery House, a well-known California mansion that was under construction for 38 years. Apparently, the widow who lived there had been told by a psychic that when the building stopped, she would die. By the time Mrs. Winchester passed away, the house had 160 rooms, 40 staircases, 467 doorways, and no blueprint. It's not an unattractive house, and the view from any given room isn't unusual, but as a whole, it's a findability nightmare.

So, after weeks of work, I flew to Washington, D.C. for a day of meetings in which I planned to present my findings and recommendations. But upon arrival, my client told me that my report had been put under embargo and my meetings were canceled. Managers were concerned that my evaluation would upset the people responsible for the web presence. I was told "it's great work, we agree with you, but the time's not right."

I was surprised and disappointed, but I felt good about the work I'd done, and I continued to work with the Library on small projects. I also reflected upon what had happened and realized there was no way to tackle the problem from where I stood. I had been hired by a middle manager who worked for one of the major service units. In such a big organization, you can't change the system from within a silo. It was painful to see the problem so clearly but have no path to a solution.

Then, months later, I was surprised again. My report had percolated through the Library, eventually making its way to the top. The Executive Committee decided it was time for the Library to change the way it works on the Web. They formed a Web Strategy Board with delegates from all major units and asked me to participate in creation of a digital strategy and information architecture. It was a massive, cross-functional, multi-disciplinary challenge and a truly exhilarating experience. And while it's too early to know if our vision will be realized, major improvements have already been made.

It's a story of success that came by surprise. But it's also a reminder that our work depends upon an encouraging cultural context. I was lucky the Library was ready for change. I know this because I've learned the hard way that many organizations are not. For instance, several years ago, I worked with a community college on their website redesign. When I talked to executives, I explained the course catalog and faculty directory were the most important and most broken parts of the students' digital experience, and I laid out a plan for renewal. Then, politely but firmly, the president told me that both were off the table. The catalog, managed by a vendor, was too costly to modify, and changing the directory might upset the faculty and their powerful union. So that was that. We restructured the whole website, quite nicely I might add, without touching its most sensitive parts.

Code is a function of culture. That's one of the most important lessons I've learned in 20 years of consulting. It's not that the tail can't ever wag the dog, but when it does, it usually happens quite slowly. That's why I balance my specialist focus on the information system in question with a generalist's eye towards the wider ecosystem. Information architecture is an intervention. It disturbs an established system. To make change that lasts, we must look for the levers and find the right fit. If we fight culture, it will fight back and usually win. But if we look deeper, and if we're open to changing ourselves, we may see how culture can help.

For example, information architects are often associated with what the Agile software community calls *Big Design Up Front*. And it's true that in the early days of the Web, our wireframes fit nicely into the sequential process of the waterfall model. We created blueprints for websites before designers and developers got involved. Many of us would have preferred a more collaborative, iterative process but were constrained by management's step by step plans.

Since then, the context has changed. While we still plan new sites, much of our work is about measuring and improving what exists. And when we do a responsive redesign, for instance, we know wireframes aren't enough, so we work with designers and developers to build HTML prototypes we can test on many devices. We've learned to collaborate with colleagues and work in diverse ways. So, at a deep level, there's no tension between information architecture practices and the principles of Agile. In fact, as an information architect, I find the *Agile Manifesto* relevant and inspiring.

Individuals and interactions over processes and tools.

Working software over comprehensive documentation.

Customer collaboration over contract negotiation.

Responding to change over following a plan.[14]

And Agile aligns perfectly with systems thinking. It's not that we shouldn't begin with a plan and a process. Both are still important. But, today's sites and services are sufficiently complex and dynamic, many eyeballs and iterations are the only way to fine-tune the whole system.

This systems-friendly philosophy also lies behind the adaptation of lean manufacturing to software. In the 1950s, Toyota figured out how to avoid the pitfalls of mass production by embracing what's now called Lean.[15] In design, all relevant specialists were involved at the outset, so conflicts about resources and priorities were resolved early on. And in production, managers learned that by making small batches and giving every worker the ability to stop the line, they could identify, fix, and prevent errors more quickly and effectively. Instead of serving as cogs in the machine, workers were expected to solve problems by using *the five why's* to systematically trace every error to its root cause. Similarly, suppliers were expected to coordinate the flow of parts and information within the just-in-time supply system of "kanban." This transparency ensured everyone knew a missing part could stop the whole system. In short, managers gave workers and suppliers an unprecedented level of information and responsibility, so they could contribute to continuous, incremental improvement. And it worked. Quality soared, and Toyota became the largest, most consistently successful industrial enterprise in the world.

In recent years, Eric Ries famously adapted Lean to solve the wicked problem of software startups: what if we build something nobody wants? He advocates use of a minimum viable product ("MVP") as the hub of a Build-Measure-Learn loop that allows for the least expensive experiment. By selling an early version of a product or feature, we can get invaluable feedback from customers, not just about how it's designed, but about what the market actually wants. It's a holistic approach that recognizes the risks of vanity metrics such as total number of users. As Eric explains "that which optimizes one part of the system necessarily undermines the system as a whole." [16] This is a lesson from Lean we can all learn from.

Both Agile and Lean are responses to complexity and bring value to the work we do. But they've grown so popular, it's a problem. For starters, there are limits to their generalization. When we see everything through the lens of software and startups, we lose our peripheral vision. Information systems aren't just code. They are also about content and culture. We must select our frame of reference very carefully, because the solution is shaped by how we define the problem.

This step is often skipped by eager teams that are ready to roll. We're in an era of imbalance where the wisdom of crowds drowns out individual insight. We need both. We should embrace teamwork, prototypes, feedback, iteration, but we must also engage experts in research, planning, and design.

We all know what it's like to learn the hard way. We never forget the time we touched the hot stove. Initially we learn by experience. But we soon realize the value of information and communication across space and time. We don't need to burn to learn. We can watch, listen, read, think, and then plan a route around pain. On my very first backpacking trip, I could head into the wilderness of Isle Royale with some trail mix and tequila, and figure out what I forgot when I need it. But my learning isn't limited to trial and error. Thanks to books and the Internet, my equipment list includes a tent, sleeping bag, stove, spork, knife, compass, flashlight, and first aid kit. Oh, and I have a highly rated water filtration system with a 0.2 micron filter that's effective against bacteria, protozoa, and parasites; because as far as learning by failure goes, it's all fun and games until someone gets larval cysts in their brain.

I'd be crazy to walk into the wilderness without learning from experts and planning ahead. The same is true when we work on the Web. The best way to avoid fatal errors is to start with a good map and plan. And while there's a role for the team in this process, somebody must take the lead. There may be strength in numbers, but understanding, invention, and synthesis occur in the individual. The term "genius design" is misleading. Nobody needs a rock star. But once in a while, we do need a mapmaker who takes the time to survey the system, uncover hidden paths and powerful levers, and share what they learn with the team. Sometimes the mapmaker must endure solitude in search of discovery, but much of this work is social. Our systems are mostly people, which means our expertise is useless without empathy. And so we study users and interview stakeholders, just as Donella would advise.

> Before you disturb the system in any way, watch how it behaves. If it's a piece of music or a whitewater rapid or a fluctuation in a commodity price, study its beat. If it's a social system, watch it work. Learn its history. Ask people who've been around a long time to tell you what has happened.[17]

As an information architect, I always begin by watching and listening, because understanding is central to my work. Clients often don't know what's wrong. Instead of solving the symptom, I dig for a diagnosis. Design is an intervention. In keeping with Hippocrates' wisdom, we should "first, do no harm." Of course, to do nothing carries risk too. So, we study and plan, but we also build and test prototypes and MVPs.

A few years ago, I worked on a website redesign for an organization whose staff was deeply divided on the subject of social media. The younger folks were gung ho. In fact, one noted "I read an article in Wired that says the Web is dead, so why do we need a site? We can do it all on Facebook." In contrast, the older managers had no time for Twitter. "I don't need to know what y'all had for breakfast" is how one executive put it. The need to embrace social media was real, but so was the fear and the ignorance.

It would have been easy to let it go, to redesign the site without social, but instead we came up with a plan of understanding and action. The first step was education. We organized a lunch lecture for the group and a one-on-one meeting for the president. In both, I explained the value of social media platforms in the context of a multi-channel communication strategy that balances broadcasting with listening and conversation.

Together, we reviewed examples to see how similar organizations were using social media, and we talked about risks and their mitigation. And it worked. When we launched the site, we also launched social. A year later, we killed the blog due to lack of time and interest. That's okay. Overall, it's a success. Staff have learned a lot about social media, and are enjoying new ways to interact with customers and partners.

When we began, social wasn't part of the plan. But, being agile, we were able to watch, listen, and respond. When we defined a social media strategy, we knew we'd get some of it wrong. But, being lean, we were ready to build, measure, learn, and repeat. We studied the system, made blueprints and plans, but were willing to launch and learn. We struck a balance that fit the context. And we chose to invest in social to create new loops, a powerful intervention that's changing the system by helping staff to learn *with* their customers.

Information architecture is an act of synthesis that leads to intervention. We must not act blindly, but analysis paralysis is dangerous too. Getting this right is important. It's not just about websites. We must work hard to understand the nature of information in systems, because our information systems change everything, even nature.

Consider the island of my adventure. Isle Royale is as remote as it gets, yet it's the subject of debate about intervention. Since its wolves are at risk of extinction, some scientists advocate "genetic rescue" to alleviate the problems of inbreeding, while others advance "wolf reintroduction" only after the population is lost.[18] Both ideas run counter to wilderness policy and the principle of non-intervention. But we're already entangled. The island is far from untouched. In prehistoric times, native people mined it for copper. Then commercial loggers took over. Now it's a national park. We aim to let nature take its course, but accidents do happen, like the dog with a virus that decimated the wolves. Plus, while moose can swim the distance (15 miles) from shore, the only natural way for new wolves to reach the island is an ice bridge, which is increasingly unlikely due to global warming.

We're also far from unbiased. It's not just that we care about nature. Many folks earn a living from the world's longest prey-predator study. There's funding from the National Science Foundation and outreach that includes books, videos, lectures, scientific papers, newspaper articles, websites, museum exhibits, art, and surveys of Michigan residents, because it may come down to a vote. These sources are neither impartial nor immaterial. Information governs intervention. It's the link that makes the loop. So it's not just about a website or an island. It's all connected. How we think about information in systems changes everything. Our ideas transform the world. We had better know what we're doing.

Literacy

I'm standing on the Iffley Road Track at Oxford University. My watch reads 6:04.20, and I'm feeling very uncomfortable. In fact, I can barely breathe. I'm in England to speak at a conference, and I couldn't resist a run on the track where Roger Bannister completed four laps in 3:59.4 on May 6, 1954 to become the first person ever to run a four-minute mile.

I was inspired by his story while training for my first marathon a few years ago. In search of running tips, I stumbled upon a book at the library called *The Perfect Mile* and was drawn in by the promise of its cover.

> There was a time when running the mile in four minutes was believed to be beyond the limits of human foot speed, and in all of sport it was the elusive holy grail. In 1952, after suffering defeat at the Helsinki Olympics, three world-class runners each set out to break this barrier. Roger Bannister was a young English medical student who epitomized the ideal of the amateur – still driven not just by winning but by the nobility of the pursuit. John Landy was the privileged son of a genteel Australian family, who as a boy preferred butterfly collecting to running but who trained relentlessly in an almost spiritual attempt to shape his body to this singular task. Then there was Wes Santee, the swaggering American, a Kansas farm boy and natural athlete who believed he was just plain better than everybody else. Spanning three continents and defying the odds, their quest captivated the world.[19]

As I read the book, I began to realize this quest was as much about information as athletics. The fact that three men on three continents were about to break the barrier at the same time was no coincidence. It's not that they ran harder than those who'd gone before. They ran smarter. Their accelerants were the modern miracles of science and publishing. In ancient Rome, elite athletes were allowed little water and no sex, and slaves flogged their backs until they bled to build tolerance for pain. In seventeenth century England, runners had their spleens removed to increase speed, an operation with no efficacy but a one-in-five chance of death. By the twentieth century however, training was getting decidedly scientific, and every advance spread quickly around the world. As a medical student, Bannister was able to benefit more than most. He didn't just read the literature. He studied the effects of training on himself. He became fluent in arterial pCO_2, blood lactate, pulmonary ventilation, and carotid chemoreceptors. And the more he learned, the faster he ran, until he broke the unbreakable barrier and earned his place in history.

A half century later, when I trained for the Detroit Marathon, there was no need to experiment on myself. My ability to use libraries and the Internet was a huge advantage. Many marathoners train by running 50 to 100 miles per week. These programs are grueling, take a lot of time, and often result in injury. I knew that wasn't for me. So I did a lot of research and found the perfect book, *Run Less Run Faster,* with a scientific training program that helped me finish Detroit in 3:08:53. I qualified for the Boston Marathon by running only three days a week. To be fair, it was hard work, and my brother supplied motivation by telling me it couldn't be done. But I would never have succeeded without finding that book.

Running is among the most natural things we do, but when we add the right information, we do it better. I find this to be true in all areas of life. When our kids ask for help with homework, I go to Google. They tell me they already searched, but I always find what we need. I succeed when they're stuck, not because I'm better at math, but since I'm better at search. The skills I learned in library school give me an edge. Whether I'm buying a car, planning a trip, or solving a health problem, my ability to find and evaluate information is invaluable.

Sadly, most people lack this literacy. Unlike "the three Rs" of reading, writing, and arithmetic which are interwoven within the K-12 curriculum, information literacy falls through the cracks. It doesn't fit into any one subject area, and teachers fail to include it in class. And it's a big problem, because the Internet makes literacy more important, not less. When I was a kid, I had a mom, a dad, and a single volume encyclopedia, and I trusted them to answer my questions. Now Google offers us billions of answers, but the difficult question is trust.

The search for truth is so tricky even librarians get lost. Evaluating accuracy, objectivity, currency, and authority is easier said than done. At the crossroads of capitalism and the Internet, it's increasingly hard to identify the interests behind the information. It's not just advertisers and politicians who spin. Even science is suspect. When we don't ask who funded the study or who stands to gain, we risk being misled. Is man behind climate change? Do vaccines cause autism? Do mammograms save lives? If we don't get better at answering, we're in for big trouble. But let's be clear. Search isn't enough. Our literacy deficit can't be addressed by consumption alone. Consider the following definition of information literacy.

> The ability to find, evaluate, create, organize, and use ideas and information from myriad sources in multiple media.

In the information age, we are all information architects. Content creation and organization are core life skills. At home and at work, from desktop to mobile, our ability to manage and make sense makes us efficient and effective. In today's cross-channel ecologies, information *is* the medium. The more we structure, the better we understand, which is important even when we're not doing the work. For instance, while executives may not organize corporate websites, they are often responsible for the mess. The CEO of a major hospital once told me she'd know the redesign was a success when folks complimented her on the website at cocktail parties. Much of what's wrong on the Web is due to such executive illiteracy.

Of course, it isn't always so easy to pinpoint the source, because the problem is deep and distributed. Remember the Fortune 500 that kept repeating mistakes in e-commerce? We were asked by the user experience group to fix the left navigation "because that's all we control." We agreed to focus on navigation if we could also tackle governance. I began my review of the website of one of the world's largest department store chains by browsing for t-shirts. And I couldn't find them. There were dress shirts and polos but no tees. I wondered if they might be too upscale for t-shirts. I almost gave up. But I dug deeper and found the root. The t-shirt link was higher in the hierarchy and easy to miss unless you already knew.

Men's Clothing
Activewear
Blazers
Coats & Jackets
Hoodies & Fleece
Pajamas & Robes
Pants
Shirts - - - - - - ▶ **Shirts**
Shorts   Casual Button-Downs
Suits   Dress Shirts
Sweaters   Polo Shirts
Swimwear
Ties
T-Shirts
Underwear

Figure 1-10. The mystery of the missing t-shirts.

Later, I asked the men's merchandiser about this tricky taxonomy. She told me they are encouraged to experiment, so a year ago she'd moved t-shirts up a level. It boosted t-shirt sales, so it was a win. I explained that while the uptick was likely due to SEO – *moving tees to a landing page made them more findable via Google* – they were now less findable for users on the site. I asked why she didn't list them at both levels. "That's a good idea" she said, and the next day t-shirts were in two places. I'm sure I earned my keep with that one small change.

But this story isn't just about t-shirts. It's an illustration of the link between code and culture. In keeping with the time-tested model of bricks-and-mortar retail, this online business is divided into departments with merchandisers responsible for sales in their sections. This model has real strengths. Each merchandiser has great freedom to experiment with product selection, promotions, page layout, and navigation; and every change is subject to metrics such as conversion rate, average order value, and net profit per customer.

But the approach has weaknesses too. While merchandisers really know their markets, they aren't well-versed in the principles of information architecture and user experience. And they are motivated by metrics to design for the local optimum. This narrow focus leads to incremental optimization that's subject to diminishing returns and leaves little room for big innovation. And it results in a site with idiosyncratic taxonomies and navigation. Search in *Men's* works differently than in *Women's* and *For the Home*. Customers must learn multiple controls and conventions. The shopping experience is disjointed and confusing, and the business wastes money on custom design and development for each department.

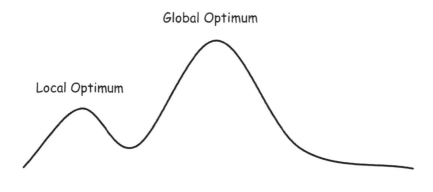

Figure 1-11. Local and global optima.

In this consulting engagement, there were lots of low-hanging fruit. As information architects, we were able to offer all sorts of ways to improve search, navigation, and the overall user experience. But these were short-term solutions to symptoms. To help our client stop repeating mistakes, we needed to tackle the underlying problem of governance. Major change to the org chart was out of the question. They were too profitable. With no crisis, there was little appetite for big change. So we suggested three things. First, establish a common platform for search and navigation to contain costs and enable a consistent user experience. Second, train the merchandisers to improve their digital literacy. And third, broaden the role of the user experience group beyond left navigation, so they can work with merchandisers on user research, holistic metrics, and design initiatives that build towards a whole greater than the sum of its parts.

These multi-level challenges are typical. It's increasingly difficult to get the information architecture right without governance. To make lasting change, we must align our information and systems with culture. This requires new literacies. It's not enough to know design. We must be fluent in frame-shifting so we can explore categories, connections, and culture from multiple scales and myriad perspectives. Archimedes once said "Give me a lever and a place to stand, and I will move the world." As systems thinkers and change agents, it's our job to look for the levers.

To some of us, this work comes naturally. We don't think in systems by choice. Our aptitudes for inquiry learning and cognitive empathy are innate. We've been tormenting folks with *the five why's* since we were toddlers. But, no matter our ability, we can always improve. If we hope to understand the nature of information in systems, we have so much to learn. Plus, frame-shifting takes practice. When we're stuck in a rut, we go soft. So we must leave the comfort of our category, again and again. Like muscles, our minds are antifragile. Stress makes them stronger. In today's fast-paced era, the ability to change is a literacy. We can get better at getting better, but only if we're willing to face our fears.

Each time I begin a project, I experience a moment of terror. My new client is trusting me with their business. They believe

I can help. But what if I can't? What if I'm unable to answer their questions or solve their problems? What if they already know what I know? Intellectually, I know these fears are unfounded. I've been here before, many times, and I always find my value. But that doesn't ease my mind. The path to peace runs through the fear. The only way out is to start.

That's why I'm so eager to begin hiking. It's the day before I'll arrive on Isle Royale. I've been planning this trip for months. Today, I have a nine hour drive from Ann Arbor to Houghton in Michigan's upper peninsula. That's a long way to worry, so I try to make it fun by playing with strange connections. I stop at Walloon Lake and reflect on Walden Pond. I've been there too. In college at Tufts one winter's night we tried mixing beer, trespassing, and transcendentalism. While breaking the law, I broke through thin ice. I had to crawl back to shore on all fours, terrorized by the crack and whoop of the frozen lake. But now, eating lunch where Ernest Hemingway spent summers as a child, I recall one of my favorite stories of his, *For Whom the Bell Tolls*, which opens with an epigraph from a meditation by the metaphysical poet, John Donne.

> No man is an Iland, intire of it selfe; every man is a peece of the Continent, a part of the maine; if a Clod bee washed away by the Sea, Europe is the lesse, as well as if a Promontorie were, as well as if a Mannor of thy friend's or of thine owne were; any man's death diminishes me, because I am involved in Mankinde; And therefore never send to know for whom the bell tolls; It tolls for thee.

When I was a child in England, my dad often quoted it to me. Even today, this poem strikes a chord, but the ring of its bell isn't wide enough, because it's limited to man. In today's flatter, fatter era of climate change, mass extinction, and lifestyle disease, "no island is an island" may be a fitter frame. To draw us together is good, but nature belongs in the circle.

Figure 1-12. Nature belongs in the circle.

Even without visible bridges, all our ecosystems are linked. That's what John Muir meant when he said anything is hitched to everything, and it's what Ted Nelson was getting at too when he wrote that everything is deeply intertwingled.

The only constant isn't change. There's connectedness too. Weaving them together to mend culture is the work of our age. To succeed, we'll need information and inspiration which means looking forward and back, as literacy is a legacy we inherit, build upon, and bequeath. Given fuzzy goals, we'll also need humor, because while frame-shifting is heavy lifting (like camping it's intense) it's also the secret to a good joke. So, let's play with categories and the occasional pun, because our destination isn't clear long after the journey has begun.

CHAPTER 2

Categories

Do I contradict myself?
Very well then I contradict myself,
(I am large, I contain multitudes.)
– WALT WHITMAN

Sitting on the floor, legs crossed, eyes closed, I watch my breath. As the air flows in and out, the unity of mind, body, and environment is clear. I dwell in the moment, calmed by concentration, inviting mindfulness. I'm aware all formations are impermanent, more sandbar than substance, and that the essence of life is dukkha, suffering, unsatisfactoriness. Inhale, exhale, the "I" fades into anattā, there is no self. The mind is at peace and open to insight, wisdom, nibbāna. In, out, a glimpse into the process of perception, a sense of interbeing, breathing towards an understanding deeper than words. And then my alarm interrupts the practice. My fifteen minutes are up. It's time to get back to work. This book won't write itself.

So, what's Buddhism doing in a chapter about classification and its consequences? Well, for starters, Siddhārtha Gautama, the person who became known as the Buddha, was an information architect. Living in India, two and a half thousand years ago, he rejected the rigid hierarchy of the caste system – the fourfold division of persons into brahmins, rulers and warriors, farmers and traders, and servants – and embraced universalism, believing enlightenment is open to all.[1] Then, he shaped several new taxonomies, including the three marks of existence, the four noble truths, the five hindrances, and the noble eightfold path. Of course, the deepest, most difficult ontology Buddha taught is anattā, non-self.

This notion there's no self – that while we're more stable than a tornado or a sandbar, we belong in the same category – is counterintuitive and disturbing, particularly to those of us in individualistic Western cultures. Self as process not substance is outside our model of the system. So while we may try śamatha, calming through mindful breathing, we're less at ease with vipassanā, which aims for "the permanent and radical transformation of your entire sensory and cognitive experience."[2] Consider this explanation of its benefits.

> You search for that thing you call "me" but what you find is a physical body and how you have identified yourself with that bag of skin and bones. You search further, and you find all manner of mental phenomena, such as emotions, thought patterns, and opinions, and see how you identify the sense of yourself with each of them. You watch yourself becoming possessive, protective, and defensive over these pitiful things, and you see how crazy that is. You rummage furiously among these various items, constantly searching for yourself – physical matter, bodily sensations, and emotions – it all keeps whirling round and round as you root through it, peering into every nook and cranny, endlessly hunting for "me." You find nothing. In all that collection of mental hardware in this endless stream of ever-shifting experience, all you can find is innumerable impersonal processes that have been caused and conditioned by previous processes. There is no static self to be found; it is all process. You find thoughts but no thinker,

you find emotions and desires, but nobody doing them. The house itself is empty. There is nobody home.[3]

If you found this passage odd, foreign, threatening, then you're ready for the upwind message we've been tacking for. Classification is as deep as it gets. It's what binds us and separates them. Understanding and behavior are rooted in taxonomy, as are religion, philosophy, reason, and ethics. Ontology is behind our senses of fairness, risk and reward, even visual perception. Categories are the cornerstones of cognition and culture. That's why it's so hard for us to grok Buddhism. We're weird. And by that I mean western, educated, industrialized, rich, and democratic ("WEIRD").

> It is not just our Western habits and cultural preferences that are different from the rest of the world, it appears. The very way we think about ourselves and others – and even the way we perceive reality – makes us distinct from other humans on the planet, not to mention from the vast majority of our ancestors.[4]

Of course, when we're not consumed by the pursuit of happiness, we too struggle with the ontology of existence. While we may have inherited the mind/body dualism of our favorite reductionist, René Descartes, who concluded the mind (or soul) can exist without the body, we need not stay bound by what Gilbert Ryle called "the ghost in the machine."[5]

In recent decades, the countervailing framework of embodied cognition has built momentum with respect to empirical research. This thesis holds that the nature of the mind is largely determined by the form of the body. Unlike computationalism, which views the brain as a central processing unit with inputs (sensory) and outputs (control), this theory of mind recognizes that how and what we think is shaped by the body's systems of perception, action, and emotion. Our bodies constrain the nature and content of our thoughts, and cognitive processing is distributed beyond our brains. In short, cognition isn't just in the head.

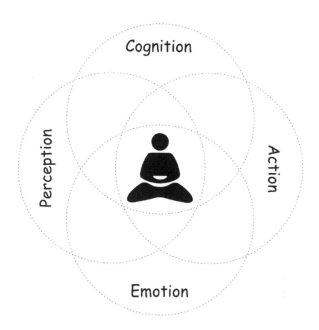

Figure 2-1. Embodied cognition.

Furthermore, according to the related theory of extended mind, thinking isn't limited to skin and skull. Cognition is shaped by and extends into the surrounding environment. When we use a pencil to sketch ideas, the pencil becomes an extension of our bodymind, and the marks we make change the course of thought. We literally think on paper. In the words of cognitive scientist Andy Clark, human cognition includes "inextricable tangles of feedback, feed-forward, and feed-around loops: loops that promiscuously criss-cross the boundaries of brain, body, and world."[6]

Our tools, like our bodies, become "transparent equipment." We see through them to the task at hand. Brain imaging studies have shown that as we build fluency, we incorporate tools – pencils, hammers, bicycles, words, numbers, computers

– into our bodymind schema. Then, in accordance with the principle of least effort, we strategically distribute work through the whole system of mind, body, environment. We use calculators for math. We offload memory to contacts and calendars. We rely on Google for retrieval, so there's less need for recall. And when we play Scrabble or Tetris, before we see a solution, we move the tiles with our fingers, because it's faster than modeling those shifts in our minds.[7]

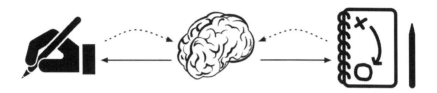

Figure 2-2. Extended cognition.

Embodiment is heady stuff, so let's explore a basic example. How about the colors of a rainbow? In school we learn the spectral colors of red, orange, yellow, green, blue, indigo, and violet are produced by the light of a single wavelength, and all are visible to the human eye, except for indigo, which Isaac Newton added so the number of colors would match the number of planets, notes in a major scale, and days in a week.

This all makes sense, sort of, until you learn that in Japan, people say traffic lights are red, yellow, and blue, even though 'Go' is green.[8] The distinction gets lost in translation since until the twentieth century, Japanese had only one word, ao, for both blue and green. It wasn't until 1917, when crayons were imported into Japan, that midori, which began as a shade of ao, was redefined as a new category, green. This split left scars, which is why apples, novices, and traffic lights are blue.

Interestingly, cross-cultural studies reveal structural similarities behind these colorful distinctions. In the late 1960s, researchers discovered that while the number of color categories varies from two to eleven, there's a common path that languages follow towards increasing specificity.[9]

Black White	<	Red	<	Green Yellow	<	Blue	<	Brown	<	Purple Pink Orange Grey

Figure 2-3. The evolution of color.

In languages with two, it's black and white. Add one, it's red. Next up, green or yellow. For six, green splits in two, creating blue. You get the picture. What's odd about this conformity across cultures is that the spectrum is continuous. There are no seams in a rainbow, and yet we see them anyway. This illusion is based in biology and refined by language and culture. The red, green, and blue cones of the human retina place a hard limit on the visible spectrum. Within that continuum, the seams we see were teased out by evolution, enabling us to distinguish food, water, and predators from their surroundings. And language is layered on top. Once we have words for colors, it's near impossible to un-see the seams.

When categories are absorbed in a culture, they become nearly as irrevocable as they are invisible. They retain power even when the ideas behind their conception are obsolete. For instance, while Cartesian dualism has been dismissed by modern philosophers, neuroscientists, and physicists, the system of Western medicine remains organized around mind/body reductionism. Doctors specialize in physical problems. Psychiatrists focus on mental disorders. In orthodox medical practice, the mind-body connection is a missing link.

I learned this myself in 2005 when I suffered terrible, chronic back pain while juggling a heavy consulting load and writing *Ambient Findability*. I first blamed poor posture and bought an ergonomic chair. It didn't help. After weeks of agony, I visited my doctor. Ignoring my hint that stress could be a factor, she prescribed physical therapy and three Advil, three times a day. I followed doctor's orders, but the pain got worse. In desperation, I went to Google with "back pain stress." I found and read a book, *Healing Back Pain: The Mind-Body Connection* by Dr. John Sarno. He argues that many musculoskeletal pain disorders are rooted in repressed emotion. To distract us from anxiety, our autonomic nervous system reduces blood circulation to specific muscles, tendons, or ligaments, thereby causing oxygen deprivation and severe chronic pain. For treatment, he suggests that patients acknowledge the psychosomatic basis and repudiate any structural diagnosis. This means no pills, no physical therapy, and resumption of all normal activity. It sounds a bit odd. But you know what? It worked. Completely. My back was healed by a book.

This experience made me see the missing link, the mind-body connection, that I'd never known I was missing. It challenged my theory of existence and raised prickly questions about our culture. Suddenly, I was unable to un-see the weirdness of Western medicine. Science and technology bring us medical miracles, but success blinds us to the dark side. The over-prescription of drugs and surgery is an epidemic. We're fixing things that aren't broken, and the cost is astronomical. For instance, seventy percent of us suffer severe back pain, and in the U.S. alone this results in tens of thousands of surgeries a year, but the herniated, ruptured, and bulging discs commonly attributed to back pain are seen almost as often in the MRIs of healthy people.[10] All too often, diagnostic classifications are made based on visible but harmless imperfections by doctors who are blind to the invisible but powerful connections between mind and body.

Of course, we're not all in the dark. Many doctors regularly prescribe placebos. They trust in the efficacy of mind over matter. And the market for complementary and alternative medicine – over $35 billion spent out of pocket each year – shows some patients grow impatient with medical orthodoxy. But mostly the $3 trillion healthcare industry rolls on.

Acupuncture	Energy Healing / Reiki	Naturopathy
Ayurveda	Guided Imagery	Progressive Relaxation
Biofeedback	Homeopathy	Qi Gong
Chelation	Hypnosis	Tai Chi
Chiropractic	Massage	Traditional Healers
Deep Breathing	Meditation	Botanica
Diet-Based	Movement	Curandero
Atkins	Alexander Technique	Espiritista
Macrobiotic	Feldenkrais	Hierbero or Yerbera
Ornish	Pilates	Native American
Pritikin	Trager	Shaman
South Beach	Natural Products	Sobador
Vegetarian	(plants, herbs, enzymes)	Yoga

Figure 2-4. Complementary and alternative medicine.

There are many reasons why medicine is a mess. Patients want a quick fix. Doctors hate saying "I don't know." And the truth is obscured by industry-funded research, advertising, and a government beholden to special interests. Marcia Angell, former editor-in-chief of the *New England Journal of Medicine* states "It is simply no longer possible to believe much of the clinical research that is published, or to rely on the judgment of trusted physicians or authoritative medical guidelines."[11]

Considering the source, that's a scary conclusion, but ending fraud won't solve the problem. Ontology is a root that runs deeper than corruption. The separation of mind-body is a category error that's hard to undo. In the 1600s, Descartes set out to validate his mechanical philosophy – the body is a machine made of parts – and to prove the existence of an immortal soul, so he wouldn't risk heresy charges from the Catholic Church and the Inquisition. Centuries later, our culture and language are subject to reductionism and dualism. The consequences of classification expand and endure.

That's why the origin of our work is ontology. Organizing for users isn't *just* about findability. In designing taxonomies and vocabularies, we serve as *architects of understanding*. We shape how users view the business, the topic, the task. For better or worse, our groups and labels endure across channels and platforms. Mega-menus designed for desktop get stuffed inside mobile hamburgers, and users are stumped. Departments conceived for retail store layouts are mapped to navigation menus on e-commerce sites, and luggage gets lost.

Our work is hard to undo, so we must resist the urge to rush. While our colleagues may run screaming from the abstraction and ambiguity of this ontological inquiry, we must have the courage to dwell in discomfort. Time spent wisely at the start of a project or journey may return dividends for years.

Of course, the start is often too late, which is why we must engage with strategy and governance. Ontology begins with the org chart. In making frameworks for collaboration, we must think about goals, metrics, roles, and relationships, because how we organize ourselves changes everything. The categories we choose and the words we use to describe the project, program, process, product, service, or ecosystem will alter the path and destination invisibly and irrevocably. A digital strategy team is blind to physical touchpoints. A user experience designer ignores content creators. A search engine optimization project ruins the information architecture. Words are the interface, not just on the Web, but in our minds. As a wise woman wrote "Language as an articulation of reality is more primordial than strategy, structure, or culture."[12]

To avoid blind spots, we must see (and speak) differently, using averted vision to shift focus from center to beyond the periphery. Imaginative re-classification reveals invisible structures, unspoken assumptions, hidden values, and novel possibilities. But it's not easy to invert the canon. Our biology, culture, education, and language all conspire to convince us there is a single, right way to organize things. Blue and green are distinct colors. History and science are separate subjects. Europe is above Africa. Books belong in fiction or nonfiction. The tomato is a fruit. Now turn the last five periods into question marks, then consider the contrary. Go ahead, give it a try. Like meditation, this intellectual yoga takes practice.

That's what we're doing in this book. By framing and re-framing, we build the mental muscles of curiosity and imagination, and we nurture our capacity to be cheeky, sassy, wise. Buddha opposed the caste system and dogma in general. He said "place no head above your own." Of course, to question the categories of custom, convention, rule, and order is to risk your neck. Galileo was found "gravely suspect of heresy" for confirming the Copernican re-classification of the universe, Joan of Arc was burned to death for "dressing as a man" and Nelson Mandela was categorized as a domestic terrorist by South Africa and the United States for defying the taxonomy – black, white, coloured, Indian – of apartheid.

Mostly what we do isn't quite so heavy. But it's unwise to ask certain questions before understanding politics and culture. In all organizations, from libraries, nonprofits, and government agencies to Fortune 500s and Silicon Valley startups, visible categories are built on invisible fault lines. So speak softly and carry some Silly String, because the dark paths that wander betwixt taxonomies and org charts are riddled with tripwire.[13]

Organizing for Users

Of course, since users are the center of our universe, it's our duty to take risks on their behalf. And while we tend to talk about the visible leaves and branches of information architecture – menus, buttons, links, labels, tags, facets, search, navigation, personalization – categories are the root of all this work. They cleave concepts and channels together and apart.

In retail, the interfaces are different – store, catalog, website, app – but the categories are consistent across channels. This accord makes it easy for users to switch systems or devices while letting managers stick to the same old org chart. But, when implemented inflexibly, users get lost. For instance, where would you look for luggage in this menu?

for the home | bed & bath | women | men

juniors | kids | beauty | shoes | handbags | jewelry

Figure 2-5. Users (and luggage) get lost.

It's a big question because suitcases and travel bags are high-margin products. In retail, luggage is among the most profitable categories. But our e-commerce client had it hidden under "for the home" because that's where it lives in the store. Users were lost – analytics showed "luggage" to be the most common search term – and undoubtedly so were sales.

The problem of lost luggage was even worse on mobile. Unable to rely upon mega-menus to reveal category maps on rollover, our client served up the hamburger icon. Beneath this visible tip of the iceberg were their invisible products, hidden under multiple choices, clicks and categories.

Figure 2-6. Most of the iceberg is invisible.

Once in the store, shoppers persist. They ask, browse, and will even use a map. Online, it's easy to shop elsewhere, so taxonomies must be tuned for findability. And it's no good responding to desktop without adapting for mobile and tablet. Stuffing categories into a big hamburger will bring bellyaches to shoppers and sellers. Users can't buy what they can't find.

While findability comes first, we must also remember that categories are about more than retrieval. Classification helps our users to understand. Through splitting, lumping, and labeling, we reveal choices and invite questions. Hardsides protect, spinners roll, carry-ons fit, and backpacks are hands-free. Which features matter most? Which bag is best for you?

backpacks | carry-ons | duffels | garment bags | hardsides

lightweights | spinners | totes

Figure 2-7. Categories reveal choices.

Of course, all taxonomies are imperfect, as is the language they're built upon. Let's say you want a messenger bag. Is that under backpacks or duffels? Or how about a lightweight, hardside carry-on with two wheels? Does that even exist? Like maps and myths, taxonomies hide more than they reveal. They bury complexity to tell a story, and they always miss someone out. Some things, like luggage, get lost by accident, while others – *people, places, and ideas* – are buried by design.

Either way, each glitch in the matrix subtly changes understanding and behavior, which is why this work often has moral weight. Classification has consequences, as Geoffrey Bowker and Susan Leigh Star argue in *Sorting Things Out.*

> Each category valorizes some point of view and silences another. This is not inherently a bad thing – indeed it is inescapable. But it is an ethical choice, and as such it is dangerous – not bad but dangerous.[14]

Taxonomies are treacherous because the easier they are to use, the harder they are to see. We grab handles without scanning contents. We trust labels without knowing origin. In the *Dewey Decimal Classification*, the system used in public libraries and taught in public schools, of the 100 numbers for religion, 88 are reserved for Christianity. Islam and Judaism each get one, while Buddhism is lucky to get its own decimal point.[15]

200	Religion	291	Comparative religion
210	Philosophy & theory of religion	292	Classical religion (Greek & Roman)
220	The Bible	293	Germanic religion
230	Christianity	294	Religions of Indic origin
240	Christian practice & observance		294.3 Buddhism 294.4 Jainism
250	Christian pastoral practice		294.5 Hinduism 294.6 Sikhism
260	Christian organization, social work	295	Zoroastrianism (Mazdaism, Parseeism)
270	History of Christianity	296	Judaism
280	Christian denominations	297	Islam, Babism, Bahai Faith
290	Other religions	299	Religions not provided for elsewhere

Figure 2-8. Religion in Dewey Decimal.

What values are implicit in this scheme? What is the intent and impact? Who does it help? Who gets hurt? What are its alternatives? And why is this the one we use? Why does it endure? We must subject all taxonomies to such questions because their imprint belies their impact. Consider, for instance, the Facebook *Like*. It's only a word, but it implies an ontology and shapes understanding and behavior profoundly.

Figure 2-9. Facebook hides more than it reveals.

Unlike *Share* or *Retweet*, *Like* nudges us into "friendly world syndrome." We have a hard time "liking" bad news, so most of the sad stories simply fade away, leaving us in a safe, happy place that's good for business. When we think about taxonomies, we tend to focus on whole systems like Dewey Decimal, but like *Like*, a single word can embody a worldview.

Words are interface and infrastructure. They are the handles that help us complete tasks and find content, but they are also symbols that represent concepts and categories. Scholars in semiotics and semantics have delved deep into the complex relationships between sign (*signifier*) and meaning (*signified*), and the extent to which that meaning is defined by intent or interpretation. One insight, extracted from the cold, dark depths of that rabbit hole, is that all words have baggage.

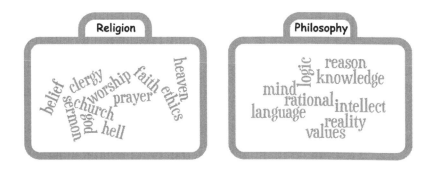

Figure 2-10. Words are handles.

Words are the interface. Hide the words, and most software, websites, and taxonomies are rendered unusable. But words are also infrastructure. They are the parts through which we understand the whole. In business, salesmen in suits are replaced by websites with words. The depth and breadth of products and services is defined by categories. In all types of organization, trust is built (in part) on taxonomy. Words that fit together are indicative of a strong mission, vision, and brand. While words play on the surface, they are accepted as tokens of substance. Experts use big words to garner authority. Politicians use small words to gain power. In taxonomies and poems, semantics is more than it seems.

Of course, half the time our words are wrong, and the consequences of classification are unintended. When we choose a word, it's packed with meaning, but lots gets lost in transit. Consider the placement of Buddhism in Religion in Dewey. The interesting question is not whether the reality of half a billion Buddhists merits more than a decimal point, but whether Buddhism belongs in Religion (or Philosophy) at all.

> The Buddha himself did not employ the concepts of religion and philosophy. These are our concepts, not his. Hence, to interpret his teaching as one or the other of these is to put it in a framework he would not have recognized. This need not mean the interpretation is simply wrong, but it may well be misleading.[16]

While Buddhism has much in common with religion and philosophy, there are meaningful distinctions. Like religion, Buddhism has rituals, beliefs, and ethics, but it is not a system of faith and worship centered around a divine being. There is no God. Buddha was a man. And like philosophy, Buddhism appeals to reason and aims for insight, but its practice of meditation seeks an understanding deeper than words.

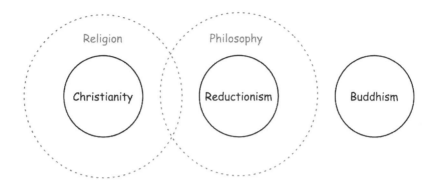

Figure 2-11. Buddhism isn't religion or philosophy.

When we use the handle of religion or philosophy, we introduce baggage. And we can't be sure of its contents, because the meaning changes from intent to interpretation. This is not a problem we can avoid. It's the nature of language and categorization. But such ambiguity begs for awareness.

On one level, when we use words to make places, the map is the territory, the word is the thing, and language is the environment where experience and exploration occur. But on another level, that's simply not true. Since understanding arises through the unity of mind, body, and environment, language can't contain meaning, or to put it poetically, in the words of Hui-neng, the patriarch of Chinese Buddhism:

> Truth has nothing to do with words. Truth can be likened to the bright moon in the sky. Words, in this case, can be likened to a finger. The finger can point to the moon's location. However, the finger is not the moon. To look at the moon, it is necessary to gaze beyond the finger.

In the systems we design, our words do lots of pointing. They serve as symbols for categories, concepts, tasks, and content. Words are necessary. They help users find what they need and understand what they find. But words are never sufficient. Meaning is irretrievably lost in translation.

Figure 2-12. Words are only fingers pointing to the moon.

As information architects, the first step is awareness of the weakness of words. Once we accept the limits of language, we go beyond them. The same is true of taxonomy. Every single one is flawed. Once we admit the problems of ontology, we solve them. Classifications, like colors, exist on a spectrum. The objective ones – alphabet, numbers, geography – are easy to use but not always useful. The subjective ones – topic, task, audience – are useful but not so easy. In the white pages, we can quickly find a friend, but it's impractical to discover a plumber. In the yellow pages, we can easily locate a theater, provided it's not called a cinema or drive-in.

The first step in taxonomy construction is defining its purpose. What's the goal? Who are the users? How will we measure success? But this isn't a linear process. A taxonomy merits Agile, not Waterfall. To put objectives before ontology is good, but we must also pair classification with context. Where will the taxonomy exist? What parts will users encounter and when? Will they touch it on mobile? Will they see it on TV? A taxonomy is part of a cross-channel information architecture. To make the whole work, we need a build-measure-learn loop that gets how the parts fit together.

Simple metrics are seductive. We move t-shirts up a level and look for a sales boost. We test and refine *within-category similarity* and *cross-category difference*, and hope for customer satisfaction. But each taxonomy has many touchpoints. Categories appear in search results, filters, facets, menus, page titles and copy, product metadata, messaging, and advertising across channels. Plus, ontologies are embodied in org charts, and vice versa. We shape our taxonomies; thereafter they shape us. For all these reasons, the detailed work of taxonomy design must be informed by the big picture. In semantics and in health, to classify without context is gross malpractice.

Years ago, I consulted with one of Canada's regional health authorities. On their site, the only way to browse was by bodily system. They'd used a taxonomy created for doctors and nurses to serve the public. And it didn't work. In our research, most people couldn't find diabetes. The taxonomy failed to meet the needs of its new audience.

Body Locations & Systems

Blood, Heart & Circulation	Ear, Nose & Throat	Kidneys & Urinary
Bones, Joints & Muscles	Endocrine System	Lungs & Breathing
Brain & Nerves	Eyes & Vision	Mouth & Teeth
Digestive System	Immune System	Reproductive System
		Skin, Hair & Nails

Figure 2-13. A taxonomy designed for health professionals.

So we added new navigation, including common conditions, an A-Z list of disorders, a symptom checker, and sections especially for men, women, teens, and kids. We used multiple ontologies in service of the objectives.

When I worked with the National Cancer Institute in the United States in 2003, wayfinding within cancer.gov was my client's objective. But I asked hard questions about findability via Google and added SEO into the mix. To serve people and search engines, we listed major types of cancer on the home page. And we enabled our human users to browse by bodily system, narrow by audience, search the full text, or consult an A-Z list. A decade later, the design has changed, the content is updated, but the information architecture remains untouched. Well-built structures stand the test of time. That's why it's so important we get ontologies and taxonomies right.

Main Nav	Types of Cancer	
Cancer Topics	Bladder Cancer	Lung Cancer
Clinical Trials	Breast Cancer	Melanoma
Cancer Statistics	Colon & Rectal Cancer	Non-Hodgkin Lymphoma
Research & Funding	Endometrial Cancer	Pancreatic Cancer
News	Kidney (Renal Cell) Cancer	Prostate Cancer
About NCI	Leukemia	Thyroid Cancer

Figure 2-14. Navigating the National Cancer Institute.

Recently, when I advised Polar Bears International, this pattern unfolded once more. Their site relied solely on main navigation. Their top level categories – programs, research, education – weren't bad. But there simply wasn't enough *infoscent* for people or search engines to follow.

So after rejiggering the main nav, we added topic and format. Instead of a "browse by topic" link, we exposed its content, and the same for format. Very few users would click "browse by format," but since everyone loves polar bear pictures, the image and video links became really popular. These changes led to a 39% increase in visits to the site the very next year.

Main Nav	Topic	Format
Our Work	Polar Bear Cubs	Images
About Polar Bears	Endangered Status	Videos
Science	Global Warming	Documents
For Teachers	Polar Bear Diet	Audio
For Students	Where They Live	
	Polar Bear Facts	
	Polar Bear Populations	
	Polar Bears for Kids	
	Adaptations	
	Hibernation	

Figure 2-15. Polar bears by topic and format.

The moral of this story is important. Due to the weakness of words, it's hard for any label at the top of any taxonomy to stand on its own. We need the root categories of main navigation so users understand the full scope, and so there's a place for all content, now and in the future. Breadth lets the system scale over time. But the top taxon is too abstract for users and the bottom too specific. The action is in the middle. So we must surface sample subcategories. Instead of burying them under *Topic*, we should bring out the *Polar Bear Cubs*.

We must reveal what cognitive scientists call "basic level categories."[17] In a taxonomy, the basic level is the largest class of which we can easily form a concrete image. It's hard to imagine furniture, but we can all picture a chair. Few people use "pinniped" or can distinguish harp from harbor, but like polar bears, we know a seal when we see one. At the basic level, we use the simple names of folk taxonomy rather than the terminology of scientific classification. They are the first categories that kids understand and have the most cultural significance for adults. Due to the idiosyncrasies of human psychology and perception, they are optimal for learning, recognition, memory, and knowledge organization. They are artifacts of embodied cognition and vital tools for design.

So far, in talking taxonomy, we've been dancing around a central point. Since every classification is flawed, we should usually use more than one. It's a simple idea that's hard to accept. We're hardwired to believe there's one right way to organize things. Dewey's classification is a monument to that spirit. But we are getting better at providing multiple maps and paths, and it's helping our users enormously. In universities, for instance, we've learned to complement the main navigation menu with alternate pathways such as audience, school, task, an A-Z index, and search.

Main Nav	Audience	School	Task
About Us	Future Students	Arts & Sciences	Apply
Admission	Current Students	Business	Visit Campus
Academics	Faculty/Staff	Engineering	Make a Gift
Research	Parents	Law	Find a Job
Campus Life	Alumni	Medicine	Contact Us

Figure 2-16. Universities offer multiple pathways.

And in e-commerce, faceted navigation is nearly ubiquitous. In the 1990s, when we began talking about facets and Shiyali Ramamrita Ranganathan, each online store had a single taxonomy, and nobody knew who he was. They still don't, but we're all indebted to the mathematician and librarian from India who realized that a single taxonomy isn't nearly enough.

14878 results for "bags"

Category	Gender	Color	Brand	Materials
Handbags (7203)	Women (11246)	Black (4241)	Adidas (14)	Leather (5442)
Backpacks (2072)	Men (3375)	Multi (1541)	Big Buddha (87)	Nylon (3441)
Luggage (1974)	Girls (136)	Brown (1361)	CamelBak (55)	Polyester (1738)
Duffle Bags (655)	Boys (112)	Blue (1214)	Diesel (72)	Cotton (841)

Price	Features	Theme	Pattern	Closures
Under $50 (2798)	Lightweight (1652)	School (1102)	Floral Print (687)	Zipper (9508)
$50 to $100 (7206)	Hardside (294)	Street (221)	Crocodile (173)	Snap (2156)
$100 to $200 (9135)	Waterproof (206)	Resort (60)	Camo (92)	Magnetic (2073)
Above $200 (3777)	Vegan (42)	Retro (43)	Cheetah Print (20)	Buckle (787)

Figure 2-17. Facets offer users a map of search results.

Faceted navigation serves up a custom map to search results that helps people understand what they've found. Users can then select filters to clarify and refine their query. Is this for a man or woman? Do you prefer black or unorthodox orange? A vegan wallet for $50? Yes, we have a few of those. Search is transformed into an iterative, interactive conversation in which users build complex queries, one simple step at a time.

And, in social, categorization is as easy as a #hashtag. Free tagging is descriptive classification without authority control. There is no hierarchy. Each tag is a category. Each object may have many tags, and vice versa. It's messy but it works. Heck, #occupywallstreet launched a movement. And event tags like #barcamp are the timely ties that bind us together.

anthropology (3,502) Apologetics (2,430) atheism (3,439) Australia (1,959) Bible (2,190) **biography** (45,961) Chicago (1,239) Christianity (7,414) cookbook (1,928) economics (9,133) essays (13,300) evolution (9,363) fiction (16,006) food (10,026) grammar (2,990) graphic novel (6,472) **history** (103,075) Holocaust (7,855) **humor** (26,499) Ireland (2,150) knitting (2,798) language (7,113) mathematics (5,461) **memoir** (52,207) mythology (6,395) **non-fiction** (224,809) **philosophy** (48,919) physics (9,765) poetry (2,499) **politics** (17,862) **psychology** (16,853) reference (16,762) **religion** (24,888) **science** (46,652) Taoism (2,129) Theology (3,837) **travel** (18,372) true crime (4,122) **writing** (16,613) WWII (14,661)

Figure 2-18. A tag cloud at LibraryThing.

Folksonomy has a light footprint, as it's hard to see the whole. The glimpse we get through clouds isn't nearly as satisfying as the view from the top-level of a taxonomy. But to fix on that contrast is to miss the point. Tagging flips the model. Rather than place each object in a hierarchy, taggers describe objects any way they want. Tag creation is idiosyncratic, bottom-up, and object-centered, and so are its use cases. The value of tags is realized in the strange connections (and descriptions) that appear once a user finds an object.

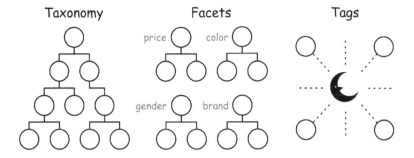

Taxonomy   Facets   Tags

Figure 2-19. Three types of classification.

Each way of organizing has strengths and weaknesses. Taxonomy affords a view from the top, facets help us muddle through the middle, and tags build bridges at the bottom. As information architects we must define the right mix for each system by balancing value and cost. And we should be open to ideas outside this ontology of taxonomies, facets, and tags.

Netflix, for example, illustrates thinking outside the box. They had a genre taxonomy and myriad forms of navigation and personalization, but they decided to make the system better.

Navigation	Genre		
New Arrivals	TV Shows	Documentaries	Music
Popular on Netflix	Action & Adventure	Dramas	Musicals
Top Picks for You	Anime	Faith and Spirituality	Romance
My List	Children & Family	Foreign	Sci-Fi & Fantasy
Recently Watched	Classics	Gay & Lesbian	Sports Movies
Search	Comedies	Horror	Thrillers
More Like This	Cult Movies	Independent	

Figure 2-20. Netflix navigation and taxonomy.

Netflix invented a unique classification scheme that blends taxonomy, facets, and tags. They built an ontological model with over 1,000 *microtags,* and hired a team of taggers to describe 14,000 movies and TV shows. Then they designed algorithms and a grammar for stitching facets and tags together into a colorful array of 76,897 *microgenres.*[18]

Microgenres

Cult Evil Kid Horror Movies	Romantic Indian Crime Dramas
Emotional Independent Sports Movies	Chilling Action Movies About Royalty
Spy Action & Adventure from the 1930s	Dark Suspenseful Gangster Dramas
Foreign Nostalgic Dramas	Visually-striking Goofy Action & Adventure
Japanese Sports Movies	Time Travel Movies starring William Hartnell

Figure 2-21. A sampling of Netflix microgenres.

Users experience these microgenres as categories. They are easy to understand and use. But there's no taxonomy. There are no subsets or supersets of *Cult Evil Kid Horror Movies.* Based on viewing history and interests, users are shown a few microgenres, each with several matching titles. It's a great way to find movies that also invites introspection and understanding, since most of us don't realize that we like *Emotional Independent Movies Based on Books* until we're told so.

Netflix has earned a sustainable competitive advantage by creating an exceptional information architecture. They got the basics right, invented new forms of categorization and personalization, and assembled these elements into a coherent whole. This is our challenge. Organizing for users is harder than we may think, and more important. Categories are the root of this work, but we should not build them before realizing their connectedness to the whole of the system. Since there are infinite ways to organize, objectives before ontology is vital, and context is the key to classification.

Making Frameworks

So, on one level, our organizational agility has improved. We have many ways to lump and split for users. But, at a higher level, we haven't absorbed this lesson by reinventing how we organize ourselves. We use tags and facets for objects, but fall back on simple taxonomies for people. John's a developer, Jane's a designer, Sara works in Marketing, and Dave is in Support. Once we split into silos, it's hard to work together.

That's why the biggest barriers in user experience aren't design and technology but culture and governance. We can't create good services without well-defined goals, roles, processes, relationships, and metrics, but all too often we oversimplify. Plan and build get split, and we fail to learn. Us and them are divided, and we fall apart. Inevitably, categorization shapes collaboration in tricky, invisible ways.

To improve these *frameworks for making* we must classify more carefully by starting to ask where our categories come from. For instance, without thinking, we build organizations on bodily metaphors. We employ department *heads* and governing *bodies* to make folks *toe* the line. And we routinely use a handful of "kinesthetic image schemas" as short-cuts.[19]

Schema	Bodily Experience	Sample Metaphors
Container	We experience our bodies as containers with boundaries (in/out).	Visual field (out of sight) and relationships (trapped in a marriage).
Part-Whole	Our whole bodies are made of parts. How they're configured matters.	Families (a marriage makes a whole) and societies (head of state, army)
Center-Periphery	Bodies have centers (trunk, organs) and peripheries (fingers, toes, hair).	Societies (middle class) and theories (the central point is most important).
Link	Our first link is the umbilical cord. We hold hands to connect bodies.	Relationships (make connections) and theories (the missing link).
Source-Path-Goal	To get our bodies from origin to destination, we move through space.	Purposes (get sidetracked) and complex events (downward spiral).

Figure 2-22. The experiential basis of metaphors.

There's nothing wrong with using metaphors, provided we're aware of their source, and realize they contain baggage that shifts from intent to interpretation. Using "department head" may induce cognitive dissonance in an organization that's flipped the org chart by practicing servant leadership. Isn't the head on top, like the upper class? Our corporeal experience is embodied in language and subtly changes how we think. This occurs all the time in our use of binary oppositions.

In-Out, Up-Down, Front-Back, Self-Other, Us-Them, More-Less, Male-Female, True-False, Fact-Fiction, Public-Private, Open-Closed, Yes-No, Hot-Cold, Reason-Emotion, Mind-Body, Man-Nature, Love-Hate, Win-Lose, Good-Evil

While there are no opposites in nature, we use dualism to create order and make sense of experience. These opposites generate meaning. We understand hot in relation to cold, light in relation to dark. This dualism runs deep. Studies show "the binary opposition is a child's first logical operation."[20] We start with self-other, edible-inedible, and work our way up to good-evil, digital-physical, map-territory. The pairings are usually hierarchical, and the first tends to be primary. It's better to be in than out, up than down, true not false, us not them. [21]

Now we sense the dangers of embodied cognition. While some oppositions appear to be self-evident, others are clearly value-laden and ethnocentric. Dualism works because it's simple, but that's also why it fails. Politicians win by painting in black and white. They say folks are either with us or against us. But this path leads to tribalism and genocide. Most horrors of human history begin with the categories of us and them.

Even when it's office politics, dualism is serious business. It divides people and obscures the truth. Is digital the opposite of physical? Is that a sensible way to split the staff? Like the Wikipedia, binary opposition can be a good place to start but a terrible place to end. Benchley's Law – there are two kinds of people in the world, those who believe there are two kinds of people in the world, and those who don't – points us in the right direction. To collaborate, we must admit ambiguity and complexity, and avoid premature classification.

For instance, teamwork is possible through greater awareness of how we (can) organize ourselves. The classic default is the bounded set of the childhood sandbox. There's a clear boundary and things are in or out. We use it because it's easy, but that doesn't make it right. Spatial ordering of physical objects isn't how ontology works. Wittgenstein famously debunked this classical theory by questioning the category of "games." It has no clear boundary as no common properties are shared by all games. Some involve skill, others luck, some you can win, others you cannot. Instead the category is united by overlapping similarities or *family resemblances*. It's hard to define a game, but we know one when we see it.

Fuzzy sets have a center and periphery. Some members are better than others. A robin is a better *bird* than an ostrich. An orange is a better *fruit* than a tomato. Madonna is a better *singer* than Bill Clinton. Terror is a better *feeling* than detachment. Most sets are bounded on the surface but fuzzy beneath. We think we can define them until we can't. In this failure lies freedom. When we admit they're not sets in stone but embodied in cognition, we're able to classify creatively.

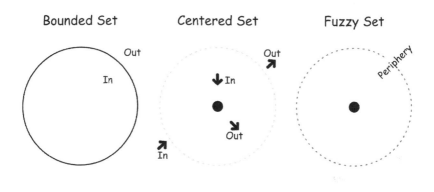

Figure 2-23. Multiple theories of categorization.

Paul Hiebert, the world's leading missiological anthropologist, did just that when he invented the concept of centered sets. His work as a missionary in India led him to ask the question "Can an illiterate peasant become a Christian after hearing the Gospel only once?"[22] By tradition, the church was organized as a bounded set with clear definitions of membership and carefully circumscribed beliefs and values. Hiebert proposed a more inclusive, dynamic way to form categories by defining a center, and by paying more attention to direction than location. In his model, a Christian is anyone who moves towards Christ. Some are closer to the center in knowledge and maturity, but all are equal members of the set. It's an ontology that values openness, change, diversity. It amps up permeability and softens the boundary between us and them.

In 2012, Dan Klyn borrowed this theory to re-frame the relationship between user experience and information architecture. In his account, using centered sets is like herding cats. The center is a pail of milk that draws cats. For user experience designers "the pail is design, and it's situated in a place where users and their experiences are the center of gravity."[23] And what about information architects? What's their center? Well, those crazy cats are centered on meaning. Or is it placemaking or planning or cognition?

To be sure, we can (and should) argue about the centers, but that's not the most pivotal point. If we connect the dots from facets and tags to fuzzy, centered sets, we begin to see the silliness of playing zero-sum games. As Schrödinger tried to tell us, a cat can exist in multiple categories at once.

There's a wonderful scene in Life of Pi in which young Pi and his mother and atheist father are walking down the street and bump into Pi's pandit, priest, and imam all together. After an angry debate, Pi is told "he can't be a Hindu, a Christian, and a Muslim. It's impossible. He must choose." In response, Pi blurts out "Bapu Gandhi said, 'All religions are true.' I just want to love God."[24] Sometimes, we must choose which story we prefer, but not always. All too often we use radio buttons when checkboxes or sliders would reveal the truth. We do it to users and we do it to ourselves.

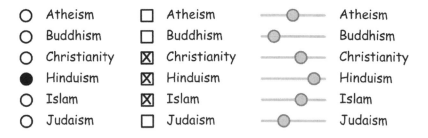

Figure 2-24. Radio buttons, check boxes, and sliders.

We can and will do better. It starts with awareness. There's more than one way to classify a cat. Once that door of perception is open, we can nudge ourselves and our colleagues towards celebrating both difference and similarity.

The org chart is a place to start. Is the hierarchy reinforcing the unhealthy division of disciplines? Might a "holacracy" of self-organizing, multi-disciplinary, cross-functional teams work better?[25] In holacracy, authority and decision-making are distributed, and members can be in more than one circle. Zappos and Medium are giving it a try. Maybe we should too.

Once the org chart's okay, layout is a lever worth a pull. Where we sit relative to our colleagues can unlock creativity and drive collaboration. While hot-desking is going too far, musical chairs reminds us we're not stuck in our seats. We shape our buildings; we can re-shape them too.

Finally, how we frame our work changes its outcome. Jane touches on this in her critique of public housing projects.

> One of the unsuitable ideas behind projects is the very notion that they *are* projects, abstracted out of the ordinary city and set apart. To think of salvaging or improving projects, *as projects*, is to repeat this root mistake. The aim should be to get that project, that patch upon the city, rewoven back into the fabric – and in the process of doing so, strengthen the surrounding fabric too.[26]

The same is true of our projects. Often they are better understood as programs or parts of systems. Historically, many of us in user experience have ignored content strategy. We neglect the people, process, and tools of the content lifecycle and everyone suffers including our end-users. When we ignore the ecosystem, our structures are certain to collapse.

Recently, I participated in an event that brought library directors together to talk about digital strategy. Lee Rainie delivered a brilliant keynote in which he presented the results of a *Pew Research Center* study aimed at learning how and why Americans value public libraries. He concluded by noting the data indicates that "libraries have a mandate to intervene in community life." [27] Later we were discussing "the vision for the library" and one participant advised the public librarians to aspire towards "a vision for the community" instead. This re-framing opened the door to an invigorating conversation about interventions and partnerships to address literacy, poverty, crisis informatics, and more. To shift mindsets from insular to open is to change the world for the better.

One shift that can help us all is to change our minds about planning. Like search, planning is a literacy that's not taught in school, and yet it's a key to success in life and work. We plan events, trips, families, sites, systems, companies, and cities. We do it all the time but make the same mistakes. First, we procrastinate. We fear complexity, so we start too late. Then, in a hurry, we split ideas and execution into phases or roles. We draw lines in our minds that segregate. The binary oppositions of think-do and plan-build are myths. Like yin and yang, these seemingly separate forces are interrelated and entangled. You can't do one (well) without the other.

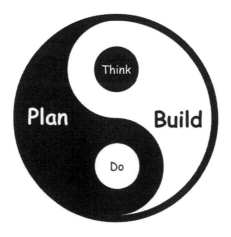

Figure 2-25. The yin-yang of idea and execution.

In planning my trip to Isle Royale, I read and made lists. But I also tried things out. In our backyard, I burned myself on the pocket stove, then learned how to foil the wind. In the living room, I modeled an "emergency poncho" for my wife. She laughed until she cried. Thinner than a dry-cleaning bag, it would have been ripped to shreds by foliage. Then she found me a real poncho. And in the bathtub, I tested the water filter, because as noted earlier, learning by failure feels like a game until someone gets larval cysts in the brain. We learn too late when we put too little do in our plan, and vice versa.

We should take these lessons online to plan-build sites and systems, because the binary opposition of agile-waterfall is just as much a myth. The Agile Manifesto backs "responding to change *over* following a plan" but makes a point of saying that both have value. Yet Agile is used often as a platform for proclaiming the wireframe is dead. Meaning shifts from intent to interpretation, and plans go out the window. We all know death by documentation sucks, but to pivot and sprint into an Agile death spiral isn't a whole lot of fun either. Fortunately, the plan-build pendulum is now swinging back to the middle thanks to a succession of expensive unplanned disasters.

The timing is good. As the complexity of our ecosystems grows, we will need plans and prototypes more than ever before. To wrangle strategy, structure, and schedule in our heads is absurd. We must put ideas into the world so we can see them. Architects have been doing this forever.

It's part of the timeless way of building that Christopher Alexander draws upon to generate the quality without a name.[28] In planning Eishin Gakuen, a combined college and high school he built outside Tokyo in the 1980s, Alexander used many tools to extend cognition. First, instead of simply interviewing students and teachers, he invited them to co-create a pattern language – a word-picture that describes the wholeness of a place – since "it is immensely hard to help people tell you what they want."[29] Together they sketched out 110 essential patterns for the campus, including:

> **2.2** The Small Gate marks the outer end of the Entrance Street. It is a small, imposing building, which has height and volume. *Hosoi, Nodera, Suzuki*

> **6.6** The Library, also a two story building, has a large quiet reading room on the second floor, with shelves, and tables, and carrels, and beautiful windows. *Kajiyama, Oginawa, Tomizu, Sato*

> **7.7** There is also one garden, so secret, that it does not appear on any map. The importance of this pattern is that it never must be publicly announced, must not be in the site plan; except for a few, nobody should be able to find it. *Hosoi*

In parallel, he and his team mapped the topography – land forms, slopes, trees, ridges, roads – of the physical site. They then began the hard work of bringing the two systems of centers, patterns and places, together into a simple, beautiful site plan. They planted hundreds of six foot tall bamboo sticks topped with colorful ribbons to identify places, spaces, and relationships. By seeing-moving these flags for months, they were able to *discover* the plan. They augmented this visualization with topographic models of the site, using pieces of balsa wood for buildings. After trial and error, they fit all these patterns and places into a wonderful, generative whole.

In this story we see the synthesis of embodied and extended cognition. There are more dimensions to architecture than Tetris, so it's even more vital we use models in the world to shift minds. Planning is making. Maps, sketches, words, and wireframes are still essential, but it's also vital that we design in the medium of construction. How else will we imagine cross-channel experiences and the Internet of Things into life?

Last year, I worked on a responsive redesign for a database publisher. Our team built wireframes and design comps to conduct quick, cheap experiments, and then an HTML prototype to enable new loops of build-measure-learn. Each of these *cognition amplifiers* is unique. Together they teach us that one way is the wrong way. As architects, designers, and developers, we each bring discrete value to think-do and plan-build. All too often, classification obstructs collaboration. It splits us and them, and our products show the seams, and our users bear the scars. The things we make are reflections of how we see and sort ourselves, so let's classify-plan accordingly, and be mindful that making frames is work.

Re-Framing

Recently, I enjoyed a tour of the *Inspired Teaching School*. It's a public charter in Washington, D.C. that cultivates inquiry-based learning by transforming the role of the teacher from information provider to "instigator of thought." Instead of showing students how to do their work, teachers challenge the kids to do it themselves. It's a tiny habit called "don't touch my pencil" that makes a big impact. The other part I recall is the artwork. I remember a colorful drawing of animals in three categories – real, imaginary, impossible – and being inspired by the freedom with which kids invent impossible creatures.

Over time, lest we're careful, our bodyminds grow inflexible. We imagine the impossible less and less until we can't. Paul Graham says entrepreneurs must be cheeky, always believing there's a better way. Similarly, information architects must be contrarians, always re-framing ideas and beliefs in a different way. Of course, Richard Saul Wurman, the infamous architect of "information architect" would beg to disagree.

> I rather worship the space between things, the silence between good friends, the time between the notes of music, the break time during a conference, the space between buildings, negative space…It's the way I approach everything. I look for a solution which has a valid oppositeness. Not a 'different way' of looking at things, but an opposite way.[30]

In fact, Mr. Wurman is so oppositional, he's easy to ignore. His own wife lovingly described his self-image as "a little piece of shit at the center of the universe."[31] But Dan Klyn is right. We must listen to our Dutch uncles.[32] It's the folks who challenge social norms that have the most interesting things to say. After all, only a contrarian would single-handedly transform the American Institute of Architects 1976 national convention into a conversation about "the architecture of information."

> That's why I've chosen to call myself an Information Architect. I don't mean a bricks and mortar architect. I mean architect as used in the words *architect of foreign policy*. I mean architect as in the creating of systemic, structural, and orderly principles to make something work – the thoughtful making of either artifact, or idea, or policy that informs because it is clear.[33]

Since that event, the borders of our practice have shifted like sandbars. We're drawn to architecture, information, planning, meaning – it seems the centre cannot hold. But that's the strength of our discipline, not a fault. We define and reframe. We destroy and rebuild. The center of information architecture is cognition. In re-re-framing, we understand.

One of Wurman's most repeated wisdoms is: "The ways of organizing information are finite. It can only be organized by location, alphabet, time, category, or hierarchy."[34] At first the last was continuum, but he changed it to make LATCH. And, in that swap, we see his scheme is arbitrary. The acronym is catchy, but it's the opposite of right. The ways of organizing information are infinite. As uncle Buddha once said, put no head above your own, because even Dutch uncles are wrong.

To build strength and flexibility, we should open our minds to people and ideas we don't like, and pick fights with those we do. For instance, Stewart Brand's concept of pace layering gets a lot of love. He argues that in complex systems, it's vital that distinct layers can change at differing rates. The combination of fast and slow creates resilience. Fast learns, slow remembers. Fast gets our attention. Slow has all the power.[35]

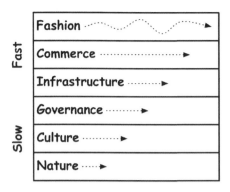

Figure 2-26. The pace layers of civilization.

It's a model he used brilliantly to explain buildings – site, structure, skin, services, space plan, stuff – and how, in time, they learn.[36] It's since been adapted widely in many fields. The order of layers affords comfort. It belies a measure of control. But all maps are traps. This is too. So, what's the opposite of pace layers? Is it everything's intertwingled?

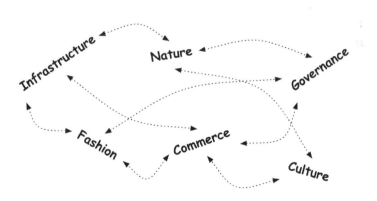

Figure 2-27. Everything is deeply intertwingled.

The layers exist. There are no layers. Both statements are true and useful. Everything depends on context. In the 1990s, the design of hardware and software as separate layers was clearly the right strategy, until Steve Jobs returned to Apple and proved the power of synthesis and integration.

We find similar opposition in our work on the Web. To define projects, managers limit by layer. We aim to refresh the interface without touching architecture. We optimize search with no content strategy. We stretch across silos, then trap ourselves in layers. To escape, we must help folks see how a simple change to a single page can send ripples from code to culture. When we limit by layer, it's vital we look for levers.

We should also look to nature for insight. For instance, coral reefs are made of layers, but that's only one way to see them. Jamaica's reefs in the 1950s served as a lovely archetype of a thriving ecosystem. Hundreds of species – sharks, snappers, parrotfish, jacks – swam among the colorful sponges and feathery octocorals sprouting from the hard coral base. In the ensuing decades, the reefs were subjected to stress and shock. Fishing and tourism grew rapidly. A fierce 1980 hurricane caused major damage. But the system appeared to bounce back. Biologists were impressed by the reef's resilience. Then, in 1983, an unidentified pathogen decimated the long-spined sea urchin population. Left unchecked, algae quickly covered and killed all the coral, and the whole system crashed.

> On a healthy reef, a new pathogen decimating a *single species* (like the urchin) might not have had catastrophic consequences, because an essential reef function – like keeping algae in check – could be performed by more than one species. On the highly compromised Jamaican reef, however, the continued flourishing of the ecosystem as a whole became entirely dependent on a single species continuing to do that job. The loss of the urchins, an otherwise modest trigger, caused the reef to collapse virtually overnight.[37]

It's vital to note that nobody predicted this chain of events. Cross-layer relationships that are easy to see *after* are often invisible *before* the event. Resilience is the capacity of an ecosystem to respond to disturbance through *resistance* and *recovery*. In our systems, we can respond better if we *frameshift* from layers to the levers that bind together fast and slow.

Tranquility or Insight

This chapter began in meditation and the search for anattā, since no ontology is more perilous than how we see ourselves. Historically, we defined man in opposition to nature, yet the boundary doesn't exist. I love our national parks, but we can't stop the clock by encircling wilderness. As Alex Steffen tells us, the future of environmentalism is *bright green*.

> Dream of living your one-planet life in a bright green city on a sustainable and thriving planet...We need, through brilliant innovations, bold enterprise and political willpower, to make sustainability an obligatory, universal characteristic of our society, not an ethical choice. We must remake the systems in which we live. We need to redesign civilization. Anything less is failure. [38]

Our old categories create externalities. We enable ourselves to cause pollution, suffering, and collapse *outside* our model of the system. But every action has an unequal and non-opposite reaction. We're dealing with karma, not physics. Man is not apart from but a part of nature, which makes the equations far more complex. It's unclear how we'll change the course we're on, but it starts with redefining ourselves.

In 2005, we added a Sheltie to our family. At first, I forbade her from the couch. But our six year old daughter Claire broke me down by tearfully proclaiming "Knowsy is a person too." In 2013, the Indian government followed suit by banning all cetacean captivity and declaring that "dolphins should be seen as 'non-human persons' and as such should have their own specific rights."[39] Now, in the United States, the *Nonhuman Rights Project* aims to reclassify animals as persons, not things.

> Our goal is, very simply, to breach the legal wall that separates all humans from all nonhuman animals. Once this wall is breached, the first nonhuman animals on earth will gain legal 'personhood' and finally get their day in court – a day they so clearly deserve.[40]

Civilization is arguably a story of an expanding moral circle. Over time, we've extended kindness from kin to tribe to nation and beyond. In 1776 when Thomas Jefferson declared "all men are created equal" he implicitly excluded women, African Americans, Native Americans, Jews, Quakers, Catholics, men without property, and anyone under 21. The Rights of Life, Liberty, and the pursuit of Happiness applied to less than ten percent of the human population. Whether we'll extend ourselves further, or not, is unclear, but shouldn't we take the time to consider our principles of classification? Is the boundary of our moral circle fuzzy or fixed? Is the center sentience or suffering? How do we circumscribe empathy? Is it emotion, fairness, or simply might makes right?

In meditation, Buddha learned everything is process, there is no self. Two and a half thousand years later, modern science is proving him right. The average age of cells in the body is 7 to 10 years, and our whole skeleton is replaced every decade.[41] A person is a pattern that doesn't exist. And it's not just impermanence that blurs what's mine. We have fuzzy borders too. The body is an ecosystem of ten trillion cells that also contains one hundred trillion bacteria that together affect digestion, weight, health, and even our mood. Each of us includes 2 to 5 pounds of them. This gives new meaning to Walt Whitman's "I am large, I contain multitudes."

We don't know our limits. Francis Crick speculated that the claustrum, a thin layer of tissue beneath the insular neocortex that has two-way links to nearly all regions of the brain, may be responsible for integrating myriad sensations – sight, sound, touch, taste, smell – into the single, unifying experience of consciousness.[42] Of course, whenever we unify, we also divide. We invent self-other as one in what Albert Einstein famously called the "optical delusion of consciousness." To make sense of an infinite universe, we create categories to reduce complexity. And we use tools and language to spread the load across mind-body-environment.

Despite these devices, our search for the truth is limited by a very small flashlight. So we must spin our categories like tetrominos. We must turn our ontologies downside-in and upside-out. We must seek monsters and cyborgs in the borderlands, and be mindful to watch for "black swans."[43] We can't make change unless we're playful, since learning means letting go. E.M. Forster wrote "the song of the future must transcend creed" and asked "how can I know what I think till I see what I say?" There's wisdom in those words, but to stare at the finger is to miss the moon.

In the beginning was yathā bhūta, reality as-it-is, unmediated by concepts or classification or culture. Now, trapped in our own maps, we meditate, in search of the untranslatable, an understanding deeper than words. We watch our breath to free our selves, to become aware of tranquility and insight, and categories and connections, as all a part of a single path.

Connections

Two roads diverged in a wood, and I –
I took the one less traveled by,
And that has made all the difference.
– ROBERT FROST

We're singing with Vienna Teng in her front yard, and we are joyful. It's the first Sunday in May, and I'm with our teenage daughters, Claire and Claudia, at the *Water Hill Music Festival*, a free, annual, all-afternoon, front porch concert put on by residents for their neighbors and the rest of the world. It's a blue sky sunshine dancing barefoot in the grass sorta day, and each of us has traveled our own path on the map of music, time, and porches, but now we sing as one people in the ancient pattern of call and response.

There'll be an evolution of the human soul (*soon love soon*)

We will know that to be a part is to be truly whole (*soon love soon*)

We will know the pattern of centuries' rise and fall (*soon love soon*)

We will know that the fate of one is the fate of all.[1]

In a bittersweet moment of *connection* we're entangled by haunting lyrics, ethereal piano, and the tie-dye caramel swirl of our own voices, and then it's all fading too quickly, a memory we share and hold dearly, like rose-lipt maidens, light foot lads, and the dawning of the age of the Internet.

Music triggers associations – intellectual, emotional, social – that tickle our brains with dopamine, transposing joy with inspiration and a sense of community, and that's what I remember about the birth of the Internet. We were in love with our newborn ability to share ideas and experiences with people all around the world. We helped one another with Telnet, FTP, and Gopher. We discovered recipes for Russian pelmeni. We built digital libraries for philosophy, beer, nanotechnology, and social justice. We were exhilarated by co-learning and co-creation, and deeply inspired by the potential of this global network to lift us up and bring us together.

Today, it's easy to get lost in the streams of Facebook and Netflix, but back then it was all about the bridges. In 1934, Paul Otlet envisioned a scholar's workstation that turned millions of 3 x 5 index cards into a web of knowledge by using a new kind of relationship known as the "Link."[2]

In 1945, Vannevar Bush imagined the memex, a machine that enabled its users to share an associative "web of trails."[3] In the early 60s, Ted Nelson coined "hypertext" and set out to build Xanadu, a non-sequential writing system with visible, clickable, unbreakable, bi-directional hyperlinks.[4]

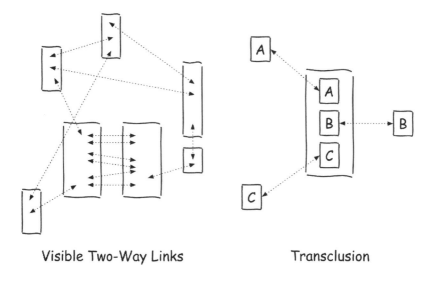

Visible Two-Way Links   Transclusion

Figure 3-1. Ted Nelson's Xanalogical Structure.

In 1968, Doug Englebart "real-ized" these dreams by showing hypertext (and most elements of modern computing) in "the mother of all demos."[5] Through the 70s and 80s, dozens of protocols and networks were made and merged, and in 1991, Tim Berners-Lee launched the World Wide Web as a public service on the Internet. The rest, as everyone knows, is history.

It's hard to argue with the success of the Internet since, and yet it's worth reflecting upon what was lost in the translation from idea to implementation. Ted Nelson did just that in 2013 in a tearful eulogy for his old friend, Doug Englebart. It opens with a pledge, "I for one carry on his work by keeping the links outside the file, as he did." The inclusion of this technical reference in a eulogy shows the depth of commitment of both men to an unrealized ideal. In all the dreams of hypertext, from Otlet and Bush to Nelson and Englebart, users were able to build and explore *shared* trails, but that's not the realized model. In HTML, authors create one-way links inside the file. This simple, modular approach helped the Web to spread like wildfire, yet it also ruled out core features of earlier visions.

Ted Nelson imagined a vertically integrated system that managed everything from code and interface to copyright and micropayment. Xanadu's transpointing windows would support bi-directional links, transclusion, and side-by-side comparison. It would elevate the work of scholars and advance Doug Englebart's dream to augment human intellect, so we might understand and resolve the world's seemingly insoluble problems. In the eulogy, Ted Nelson makes clear the heights of their ambition and their depth of disappointment.

> I used to have a high view of human potential. But no one ever had such a soaring view of human potential as Douglas Carl Engelbart – and he gave us wings to soar with him, though his mind flew on ahead, where few could see…And here we twiddle in a world of computer glitz, as the winds rise, and the seas rise, and the debts rise, and the terrorists rise, and the nukes tick.

Now I appreciate Ted's perspective, and I find his honesty refreshing, but I choose the confusion of hope over the clarity of despair. I don't see the success of Steve Krug's *Don't Make Me Think* as a condemnation of human nature. The simple solution won because most people are too busy thinking to think about interface design and information structure. We're not too lazy to play Englebart's violin[6] but are simply preoccupied with our own ways of making music. And while civilization may be headed for collapse, it's not too late for course correction. That's why I care about the Web. It's not only a mirror but a lever as well. And while today's Web is more terrible than ever imagined, it's also more amazing.

Ted Nelson invokes our past sense of possibility and asks us to imagine the Web that might have been if only we'd traveled a different road. It's not a bad way to spend time, but only if we dedicate ourselves to the divergent, forking paths ahead, because it's what we do next that makes all the difference.

Links

The core feature of the Web is the link. Likes and keywords are important too, but social and search at scale would fail without links. It's the links that make a web, yet we spend our time on interfaces, designing the surface without analyzing the structure. This is a shame. The richness and diversity of link types is rising, but to benefit we must pay attention.

Initially, we fixed on navigation, and our maps and paths remain vital for mobile and cross-channel design. We use links to forge paths for users. They serve as *transparent tools* for people who are too busy doing something to pay attention to what they're doing. The link is like a pencil or a hammer. In the words of Martin Heidegger, each tool is invisible, implicit, and *ready-to-hand*. But users do get stuck, so we use links to make maps as well. Our menus and taxonomies are visible, explicit, and *present-at-hand*. They demand our attention in return for understanding. This is almost always not a bad deal.

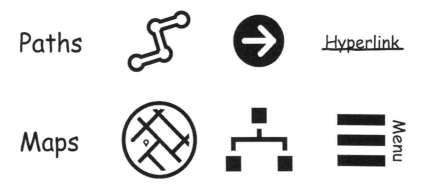

Figure 3-2. We use links to make maps and paths.

Since recognition is easier than recall, search is no substitute for words on the screen. As Marcia Bates illustrated long ago, the process of seeking is iterative and interactive, more berrypicking than math.[7] What we find and learn changes how and where we look and who and what we seek. To information foragers who satisfice in patchy environments, words are the signs and scent.[8] Words as links invite choice and inspire confidence, letting us know we're on the right path. As we may think, the map is the territory, and the paths and places we build with links are physically real.

Search increases precision at the expense of serendipity. It also reminds us that navigation isn't the sole lens for links. In the eyes of Google, links are votes. In the aggregate, they reveal structures invisible except at scale. Of course, links take us outside the frame of findability. Is the link useful, usable, accessible, credible, and desirable? Must it be <u>blue</u> or might it be better as a button? How about an icon with hover text, or a full-blown mega-menu? And what about mobile? Code, content, design, and brand offer diverse ways to understand that a link affords more than a click.

While one-way is the norm, our systems host many link types. Links open tabs, windows, media players; make phone calls, run queries, launch apps. While trackbacks aren't mainstream, we use analytics and referrer logs to monitor backlinks. We want to know who links to us. On Kindle, popular highlights become shared links, revealing the passages we respond to the most. In tweets, #hashtags aren't only links but categories and comments as well. User names are bi-directional. Maybe that's why *@TheTedNelson* is on Twitter.

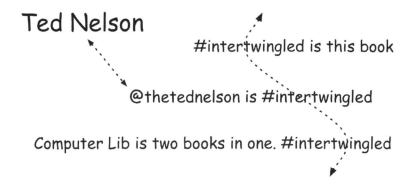

Figure 3-3. N-directional links on Twitter.

If you look deeper, you'll see triples – subject, predicate, object – defining semantic relations as precisely as possible. In ontological experiments, domain-specific models of entities, relationships, and attributes push the limits of information visualization and knowledge discovery. We're on the verge of teaching systems to make links that uncover new questions.

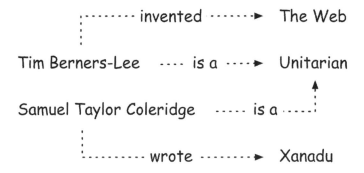

Figure 3-4. The Semantic Web is built on triples.

Of course, links aren't limited to digital networks. A book affords random access with its index and citations. A park links places with signs, paths, and bridges. And, off course, we may need a table of contents or a map or a metaphor, so we might know where we can go from where we are. As Richard Saul Wurman says "we only understand something relative to something we already understand," and this only grows more important as we orchestrate cross-channel services. In shops, barcodes and URLs serve as links to product details and the endless aisle. In airports, mobile phones let us check in, swap seats, find gates, and make connections we'd never have made before. The rollout of cross-channel services is fast and near invisible, so we need paths and maps to help us see what's possible. As Andy Polaine suggests in *Service Design*, the space-time "in between" deserves more of our attention.

> It is much easier to focus design effort on the boxes because they represent tangible touchpoints – the website, the ticket machine, and so on – but most people forget to think about designing the experience of the arrows, which are the transitions from one touchpoint to the next.[9]

Links afford movement in space and time and help us make what we can barely imagine. In augmented reality with a heads-up display, places are links to people, content, and services. We must be careful where we step. And in the Internet of Things, objects are links to their own stories, spime that may change culture by absorbing externality. The service evidence of folded toilet paper is but a sign of things to come.

As discrete products shift into service ecosystems, our information shadows grow, and so do complexity and confusion. We will need the limits of paths, the myths of maps, and the serendipity of ourselves to make sense. We will also need a remembrance of things past, from transclusion to transpointing windows, since meaning is lost in translation, and memory isn't nearly as reliable as seeing connections side by side. In the futures of user experience and service design, the architecture of cross-channel links is critical. The boxes still matter, but it's the arrows that amplify their consequence.

Loops

The business theorist Karl Weick tells managers to shift from nouns to verbs, from organization to organizing. We'd do well to heed his words. As information architects, we must marry our passion for structure and semantics with an appreciation for the causal arrows of time. We might begin by dusting off old diagrams, asking what each map is made to show and hide. For instance, a process flow makes it look simple, defining major actions and decisions as steps, but the linearity may be deceptive, its purpose to hide politics and mess.

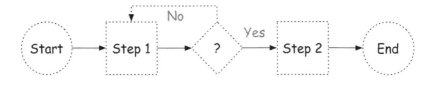

Figure 3-5. A flow diagram shows tasks and decisions as steps.

A Gantt chart gets us on schedule, making deadlines and dependencies our aim. It shows concurrency nicely, but quality may go down the drain.

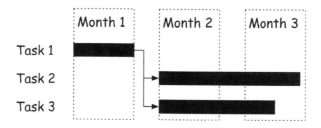

	Month 1	Month 2	Month 3
Task 1			
Task 2			
Task 3			

Figure 3-6. A Gantt chart shows deadlines and dependencies.

When we're ready to dig deeper, the "fishbone diagram" can facilitate root cause analysis. To begin, we define the problem and its major causal categories, then brainstorm the branching sub-causes by asking *five why's*. Fishboning helps us to improve quality and understand cause-and-effect, but it rarely tells us precisely where to fish or swim next.

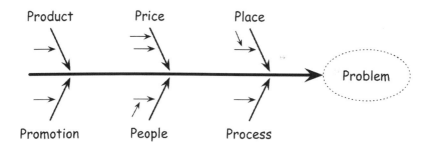

Figure 3-7. A fishbone diagram shows cause and effect.

The stock-and-flow gets us thinking about the inputs, outputs, loops, limits, and delays behind oscillation, equilibrium, and resilience. It's useful for prediction and analysis, to see where systems may go wrong, but it's too complex for most folks and vulnerable to the black swan.

Inflow (Control)   Stock   Outflow (Control)

Figure 3-8. A stock-and-flow shows controls and context.

Each diagram is useful, but all maps are traps; that's why we need more than one. By mixing models we paint a picture that helps us see the truth. We've done this with spatial maps, but it's time to tackle time. Business is stuck at the surface. Managers pretend measurement is simple and clear: set goals, track progress, reward success. But that's not how it works. The loops that bind goals, process, and metrics are very tricky.

The story of how we work and what we count is told by the faults in our products and the seams in our services. Today's shallow, siloed analytics will not stand. Of course we should measure clicks and conversions, but fixation on feedback loops that are easy to see is reminiscent of the drunk seeking his car keys under the streetlight. What's lost in the chatter about KPIs (*key performance indicators*) and OKRs (*objectives and key results*) is the value of insight and synthesis. Should we survey customer satisfaction and loyalty? Absolutely! Can the practice of making public commitments to ambitious, measurable goals boost motivation and performance? Yes!

But we must be wary of reductionism and recidivism. Our numbers tell us *what* but not *why*; they calculate the future as the sum of its past; and shape how we think and what we do more than we know. Once a metric is defined, it's hard to ignore. If we use conversions as a metric, satisfaction and loyalty may suffer. When we commit in public to a goal, we're less likely to pivot. It's our conversations about the numbers that count. Right action follows the whole of *what* and *why*.

Peter Drucker, the legendary management consultant, is credited with the maxim "if you can't measure it, you can't manage it," but he was far too wise to say that. The truth is self-evident in his advice to an executive.

> Your first role...is the personal one. It is the relationship with people, the development of mutual confidence, the identification of people, the creation of a community. This is something only you can do. It cannot be measured or easily defined. But it is not only a key function. It is one only you can perform.[10]

These are the questions we must ask. What's important but can't be measured? Is it being ignored? What's the something only you can do that's not being done right now? Is it time for you to act? I'm hopeful we will make connections that make a difference by shining our light into the darkness beyond the streetlamp. To sketch links and loops out of thin air is to make the invisible visible. It's a power we must use responsibly, since the lines we draw are harder to erase than we may think.

Our interventions in complex systems beg for humor and humility. We are all butterflies, flapping our wings, no idea of the chaos we cause. In physics and ecology, complexity limits prediction, and that's without the multiplier of mankind. Our plans are not only subject to butterflies but to the cobra effect as well. In colonial India, the British government tried to reduce the number of venomous snakes in Delhi by paying cash for dead cobras. It worked for a while until people began breeding cobras, then the government killed the bounty, and breeders set their snakes free. Our actions may achieve the opposite of our goals especially when humans are involved.

Pads and helmets made football a more dangerous sport. Censorship generates enormous publicity. Iatrogenics, adverse effects from medical treatment and advice, is the third leading cause of death in the United States; a visit to your doctor may kill you. Of course, perverse incentives are partly to blame, but it's messier than that. People are hard to predict. We make mistakes. We're bad with numbers. We're surprisingly irrational. And we imitate each other, so ideas and behaviors, good and bad, spread like wildfire. In short, people make complex systems even more weird and unpredictable.

Years ago, I redesigned the information architecture for a philanthropy. Stakeholder interviews confirmed the main goal of the website was to help aspiring grantees apply for funding. User research suggested that grant seekers were frustrated that critical data about opportunities and deadlines was scattered around the site. I had an idea to create one new page with a simple table to show "what's open when" across all the program areas of the foundation. This *Apply for a Grant* page was a big hit with users, becoming the second most visited node after the home page. However, not long after launch, the Board of Trustees noticed the table, and they were shocked by the number of programs that were not accepting applications.

This made waves in the organization. There was talk of removing the page. Then a few programs changed status from closed to open, suggesting that the tail might wag the dog. Then I heard that wasn't true. Those programs weren't truly open. Fortunately this didn't last long, and transparency won the day. The philanthropy clarified itself, explaining that its strategic approach to funding obviates the need for unsolicited applications in several areas. Managers already know who's who in their community. They invite applications, advance collaborations, and make investments accordingly.

Users   Stakeholders

Figure 3-9. Information changes organizations.

The ripples made by this pebble were fascinating. A modest change to the information architecture brought strategy and culture into question. I'm pleased by the introspection it led to, but I can't take credit as it wasn't my goal. Surprises in life are more common than most of us care to admit.

One reason we make mistakes is known as the problem of induction. We spend our lives trying to see the future using our knowledge of the past. We draw general conclusions by observing specific events. Induction is the root of how we know what we know, and it works surprisingly well, until as Nassim Taleb explains, we find we're the turkey, not the swan.

> Consider a turkey that is fed every day. Every single feeding will firm up the bird's belief that it is the general rule of life to be fed every day by friendly members of the human race "looking out for its best interests," as a politician would say. On the afternoon of the Wednesday before Thanksgiving, something unexpected will happen to the turkey. It will incur a revision of belief.[11]

This reminds me of the J. C. Penney link spamming scandal. The retailer hired a search marketing firm to improve its ranking in Google; and they got great results. Month after month JCP was the top search result for such queries as "samsonite carry on luggage" and "little black dress." Executives were happy and well fed until the *New York Times* exposed the black hat campaign behind their results, Google banished them, and they discovered they were the turkeys.

Years later, JCP still fails to make Google's first page except by paying for ads. Relying on results from a black box is foolish. Don't trust that it works. Ask why. When we understand, we increase our ability to manage events. We can change tactics or plan a response. But we can never fully escape the limits of induction. That's the moral of the story of the lucky farmer.

> One day the farmer's horse ran away. His neighbors cried "such bad luck" to which he replied "maybe." His horse returned the next day with three wild horses. His neighbors shouted "that's wonderful" and the old farmer replied "maybe." The next day his son rode one of the wild horses, fell off, and broke his leg. The neighbors called it a "terrible misfortune." The old man replied "maybe." The day after, the army came to the village to draft young men, but the son was spared thanks to his broken leg. The neighbors said the farmer was lucky how things turned out, and the old man answered "maybe."

It's impossible to predict the future, yet we do it all the time. We nod at the wisdom of the Zen farmer, then proceed with business as usual. We make plans, take steps, and get angry when things go awry. Awareness isn't ambivalence. We care about outcomes, and to some degree we are in control. Prediction helps us to see the future in more ways than one.

> Prediction is so pervasive that what we "perceive" – that is, how the world appears to us – does not come solely from our senses. What we perceive is a combination of what we sense and our brains' memory-derived predictions.[12]

As Jeff Hawkins explains, the simple act of opening a door is built on prediction. Memory enables us to open our front door without thinking. We predict what will occur when we turn the knob and push. If the door is stuck and our prediction proves wrong, then our attention turns on, and we start asking questions. Much of what we "see" is based on what we expect. As the neuroscientist V.S. Ramachandran explains:

There are at least as many fibers (actually many more!) coming back from each stage of processing to an earlier stage as there are fibers going forward…The classical notion of vision as a stage-by-stage sequential analysis of the image, with increasing sophistication as you go along, is demolished by the existence of so much feedback.[13]

This explains our susceptibility to optical illusions and the fallibility of eyewitness testimony. The truth lies in between "seeing is believing" and "believing is seeing" and this prediction isn't only about eyesight.

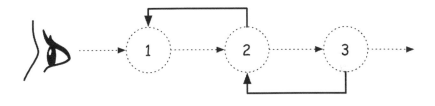

Figure 3-10. In vision, there's more feedback than input.

Music, management, and imagination are all about prediction. A song tickles us by surprise, managers count on cause and effect, and we dream in folded feedback, exploring the consequences of our own predictions. Anticipation is behind all we think and do. In the words of Jeff Hawkins, "Prediction is not just one of the things your brain does. It is the primary function of the neocortex and the foundation of intelligence."[14]

It's impossible *not* to predict the future, yet we get it wrong all the time. We use our "theory of mind" to anticipate the actions and reactions of colleagues and customers, but people are full of surprises. Experiments help, but induction has its limits. Even minimum viable products can't predict the long now at scale. Inevitably we must move forward, often at a fast clip, but it pays to be aware of error even as we race along. Often our mistakes are small, obvious, and easy to fix. It's the big ones we must look out for. They're not only hard to correct but amazingly hard to see. Chris Argyris, a pioneer in organizational learning, had it right when he advocated double-loop learning, a concept he introduces by analogy.

> A thermostat that automatically turns on the heat whenever the temperature in a room drops below 68 degrees is a good example of single-loop learning. A thermostat that could ask, "Why am I set at 68 degrees?" and then explore whether or not some other temperature might more economically achieve the goal of heating the room would be engaging in double-loop learning.[15]

Of course, double-loop learning in organizations is rare. Defensiveness in cognition and culture makes it hard to question basic beliefs. Successful people and organizations are the worst, as they've never learned to learn from failure. Experts and executives alike deny the problem, shift blame, and shut down; and the organization runs efficiently off a cliff. We can get better, but it takes commitment. We must confront the assumptions behind our ideas. We must surface conflicting opinions and recast them as hypotheses to be tested in public. And we must be willing to critique and change our goals, values, frameworks, policies, and strategies.

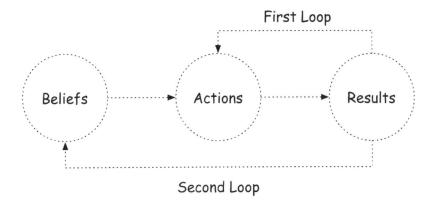

Figure 3-11. The two loops of double-loop learning.

In short, we must go deep, breaking the icy surface in search of the truth. This reminds me of Robert Frost's *The Road Not Taken*, a poem I've loved since high school, and a source of inspiration in my decision two decades past to take the road less traveled by becoming an information architect. Of course, the joke's on me. A few years ago, while helping our daughter with homework, I searched for "road not taken meaning" and found "in leaves no step had trodden black," I'd been wrong all that time. No road is less trodden, and that truth is revealed with a sigh. Frost dropped hints and warned us explicitly.

You have to be careful of that one; it's a tricky poem – very tricky.

But, inspired by his words, we missed his meaning. We chose our roads less traveled, knowing that made all the difference. One can only imagine the unintended consequences of this mass misinterpretation. As for me, I love it all the more as the poem about forks that took me for two loops.

Forks

In 1941, Jorge Luis Borges, a blind Argentine librarian, wrote an amazing story, *The Garden of Forking Paths*, about a book and a labyrinth containing "an infinite series of times, a growing, dizzying web of divergent, convergent, and parallel times...all possibilities." This use of analogy to connect the forks of space and time is poetic, irresistible, and recursive.

In 1991, Herbert Simon, the polymath pioneer of artificial intelligence and decision theory, wrote "I have encountered many branches in the maze of my life's path, where I have followed now the left fork, now the right. The metaphor of the maze is irresistible to someone who has devoted his scientific career to understanding human choice."[16]

It's a powerful metaphor, but all maps are traps. While divergent paths may seem obvious in hindsight, they aren't easy to see in advance. All of our decisions are made without a complete understanding of the options and consequences; not that we don't try. Our brains routinely imagine choices and outcomes, and when the possibilities are too fuzzy, we stall.

We muddle around in a state of productive procrastination, and while muddling can be hard to defend, it's precisely the right thing to do. We must buy time to find our way, because the relationships between choice, action, and cognition are far messier than we like to admit; and once we step from the handle to the tine, there's no going back. Perhaps the utensil that affords the wisest decisions isn't a fork but a spork.

Figure 3-12. Choose your fork carefully.

Nobody understands the trickiness of decisions better than Karl Weick, but in explaining his perspective, it's hard to know where to begin. Like E.M. Forster, Weick invites us to consider the effect of action on cognition by asking "how can I know what I think till I see what I say?" He argues that *retrospective sensemaking* is more common than we know. We act first, then rationalize our aim, but prediction is part of it too. In organizations, the basic unit of sensemaking is the double interact. An interact exists when an act by Person A evokes a response by Person B. A double loop is created by A's reaction to B's response. This is how meaning is made.

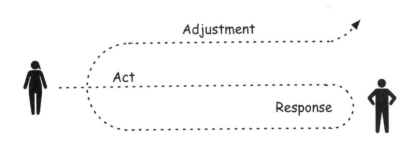

Adjustment

Act

Response

Figure 3-13. A double interact loop.

The first act is shaped by models we've built to make sense of the past. In Weick's words, our thoughts are "real-ized" as self-fulfilling prophecies.

> I mean literally that people make real, or turn into a reality, those ideas that they have in their heads. It is that sense in which the phrase "believing is seeing" is more than a play on words.[17]

But, after that initial action, our sensemaking is complicated by commitment.

> When people take actions that are visible (the act clearly occurred), irrevocable (the act cannot be undone), and volitional (the act is the responsibility of the person who did it), they often feel pressure to justify those actions, especially if their self-esteem is shaky...thus, commitment, like metaphor, can be an enemy of wisdom. Both of them minimize doubt and doubting.[18]

I'm reminded of a comment by Scott McNealy, the outspoken co-founder of Sun Microsystems and its CEO for 22 years. After a lecture at Stanford, when asked how he made decisions, he responded by saying in effect "It's important to make good decisions. But I spend much less time and energy worrying about making the right decision and more time and energy ensuring that any decision I make turns out right."[19]

There's insight in those words but danger too. Wisdom requires a balance between confidence and caution. Sun failed to see the shift from hardware to software and was acquired by Oracle. For double loop learning, we must first admit error, something Bill Gates does well. After the Gates Foundation spent $2 billion to replace large schools with small ones and realized only modest gains, Gates publicly concluded they'd made an expensive mistake, and decided to switch direction.

In *Mistakes Were Made (But Not By Me)*, we're reminded such honest admissions are refreshing because they're so rare. The main problem isn't that we aim to deceive others; it's that we fool ourselves. The engine of self-justification is cognitive dissonance, the state of tension that occurs when we hold ideas or beliefs that are psychologically inconsistent. If a "good person" does a "bad thing" self-deception kicks in. And, if on opposite sides of a decision, time will tear us apart.

Imagine two students with similar attitudes and abilities who struggle with the temptation to cheat on a test. One yields and the other resists. How do they feel about cheating a week later? The first tells herself it's no big deal, whereas the second decides it's totally immoral. In time the two slide further apart, until the cheater and do-gooder can't stand each other. They began together but were polarized by the *pyramid of choice*.[20]

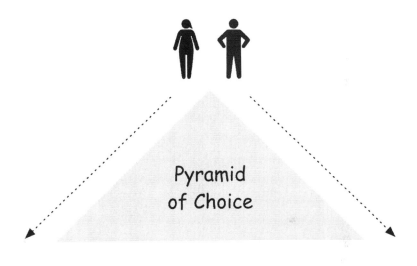

Figure 3-14. Separated by self-justification.

Retrospective sensemaking is an invisible yet powerful force in our lives. As Karl Weick suggests, when *what* precedes *why*, it's impossible to undo.

> People need to be less casual about action since whatever they do has the potential to bind them and focus their sensemaking.[21]

That's why we must make time and space to explore before we act. As Dave Gray explains, in knowledge work our goals are fuzzy, creativity is vital, and the path to success is not a straight line. In *Gamestorming*, he presents the shape of innovation in three acts. [22] Act one is divergent. We open minds and expand options with optimism and freedom. Act two is emergent. We explore by seeking patterns, testing prototypes, and trusting serendipity. Act three is convergent. We employ synthesis and evaluation to come together and make a decision. Dave sketches this process – open, explore, close – as a stubby pencil sharpened at both ends, but in my mind it's a spork with space-time between the handle and tine.

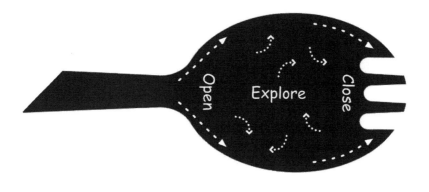

Figure 3-15. The spork of innovation.

Either way, there are three acts before the act that commits. It's okay if the iffiness is visible. Agile and Beta made it safe to experiment in public. The thing to be aware of is irrevocable, a word that means you can't go back. In *Antifragile*, Nassim Taleb promotes "optionality" as a way to benefit from the positive side of uncertainty. [23] It's best to keep our options open, since information and intelligence are often no match for wait and see. Anyone who's watched *House* has seen applied optionality in the sequence of symptom-treatment-diagnosis; it's a strategy Karl Weick prescribes.

> When physicians make a formal diagnosis under time pressure, their rush to label the disease, begin treatment, and achieve closure leads them to overlook and then forget symptoms that don't fit the diagnosis. This encourages more confidence than may be warranted...A hunch held lightly (that is, without commitment) is a direction to be followed, not a decision to be defended.[24]

The act of labeling merits attention in all the work we do. Like maps, words are traps. We must speak carefully since we think what we say. The order of operations makes a difference; that's why process is key. Recently, I worked on a prototyping project in which we purposefully created wireframes and design comps in parallel. In weekly reviews, we'd flip back and forth, at times asking questions we'd already asked.

Interestingly, the answers sometimes changed. When I first suggested we merge Save Search and Save/Share Results, our client defended their existence as separate features. But a week later, we revisited the same interface, and once again I made the case for convergence. A single *Save/Share* menu button makes it impossible to choose the wrong option and helps users to learn about related features. And this time our client agreed. I'd had time to clarify my argument. Our client had time to get used to the idea. Also, it was a less hectic meeting, and the group was receptive to change. This collaboration took time and was messy. We'd pick a road in the fork only to loop back around. But this process improved quality enormously. By creating a safe space-time in which actions and decisions aren't binding, we defused self-justification for a while.

Of course, we often lack the luxury of space-time. This limits collaboration and the scientific method. When thorny questions arise, folks love to suggest A/B testing. Sometimes that's a great idea, but often the complexity and connectedness of the system make it unfeasible. It's difficult to isolate variables, and we can't always judge long term efficacy based upon the initial response. Users adapt to change over time. Also, creating dual designs that integrate into the whole takes a lot of effort. Eric Raymond argues that *forking* is a taboo of open source culture and almost never happens.

> There is strong social pressure against forking projects. It does not happen except under plea of dire necessity, with much public self-justification, and with a renaming.[25]

The right to fork is an important freedom of open source, but it's also a last resort. Both child projects have fewer designers and developers; and once done, it's impossible to undo. While it's pretty to think so, we truly can't explore parallel universes. It's simply not possible to put all your energy and resources into both sides of an A/B test. In reality, we often must *satisfice* with imperfect information. This is where strategy can help.

To outsiders, a company's actions and acquisitions can appear chaotic, but behind the scenes it may all make sense. For instance, Walt Disney built a sprawling empire, but each asset fit strategically in his map.[26] He knew how the parts made a whole and never made decisions in the dark.

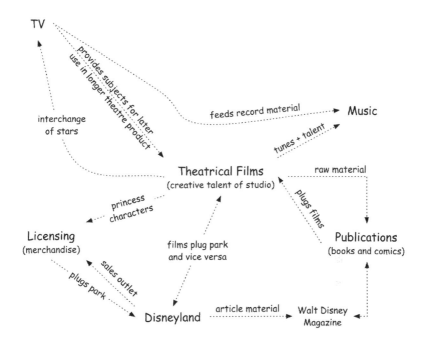

Figure 3-16. Walt Disney's Theory of the Firm.

There's a similar story behind Southwest Airlines. It began as a triangle on the back of a napkin with direct routes between Dallas, San Antonio, and Houston.[27] But the simple plan to ditch hub-and-spoke soon evolved into a textbook case of what Michael Porter calls *strategic fit*.[28]

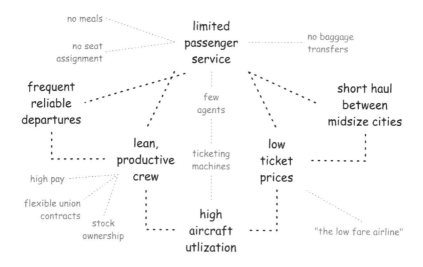

no meals

no seat
assignment

limited
passenger
service

no baggage
transfers

frequent
reliable
departures

few
agents

short haul
between
midsize cities

lean,
productive
crew

ticketing
machines

low
ticket
prices

high pay

flexible union
contracts

stock
ownership

high
aircraft
utlization

"the low fare airline"

Figure 3-17. The "Fit" for Southwest Airlines.

First, there's simple consistency between each activity and the overall strategy. Second, the activities are reinforcing. Third, the system allows for an *optimization of effort* that makes the whole greater than the sum of its parts. Fit's hard to decipher without a key, so competitors can't copy, and we're more likely to enjoy sustainable competitive advantage. Plus, once we've done the synthesis needed to make the map, decisions are easier. We know why and where each part belongs, and we're able to balance local maxima with optimization of the whole. Dig deep into any successful organization, and you'll find the fingerprints of a leader who understands the art of connection; it's built into every link, loop and fork.

Reflection

The oldest known musical instruments, flutes made of bird bone and mammoth ivory, are roughly 40,000 years old, but our tribal ancestors were singing, whistling, and tapping their hairy toes long before that. Music isn't apart from us but a part of us. Its cross-modal power to trigger social, emotional, and intellectual associations isn't incidental. From beat to lyrics, music, poetry, and metaphor have played instrumental roles in the co-evolution of our mind-body-environment. In *The Tell-Tale Brain*, V. S. Ramachandran connects the dots between creativity, synesthesia, and the architecture of the brain.

> In biological systems, there is a deep unity between structure, function, and origin. You cannot make very much progress understanding any one of these unless you are also paying close attention to the other two.[29]

I recall learning my mum sees letters, numbers, and words in color. B is dark blue. 7 is pale green. Monday is cream yellow. We all had a laugh at her craziness. Years later, we discovered she had a rare neurological disorder known as synesthesia. To some synesthetes, the touch of denim is sadness; for others, C-sharp on a piano is blue. She was still crazy, but she wasn't alone. Then synesthesia became popular. Studies revealed cross-sensory perception to be surprisingly common among artists, poets, and musicians. Suddenly, everyone and their mother was a synesthete. And, according to Ramachandran, that's not far from the truth. We are all on the synesthesia spectrum. The neural linking of color and emotion is an evolutionary adaptation for finding ripe berries, and our proclivity for synesthesia is an exaptation layered on top of that. "The angular gyrus may have originally evolved for mediating cross-sensory associations and abstractions but then, in humans, was co-opted for making all kinds of associations, including metaphorical ones."[30]

The ability to use analogy is the root of creativity, and like the future, it's unevenly distributed. We all see the road not taken isn't really about a road, but its meaning is missed by many, and its artistry is the domain of the few. We will invent the Web ahead by making cross-modal connections in our mind-body-environment. That's what we all missed in our original vision in a dream of Xanadu. To augment human intellect isn't enough. Action, emotion, and perception are part of it too.

Hypertext is a place to start, but one-dimensional links are a trap. To escape flatland, we must expand awareness. As information architects, we must identify and use invisible connections in space and time. To build places made of information is exciting, but it's not the point. We must also rise to the challenge as architects of individual, organizational, and environmental synesthesia. We must make links, loops, and forks into levers for positive change. Cross-channel isn't enough. The systems of the future are cross-sensory. It's time to design and experience new forms of connectedness.

There's a reason systems thinking isn't popular. It's too hard. In place of understanding, most folks rely on culture, which not only tells us which road to take, but also that it made all the difference. Culture is a powerful, hidden force, highly resistant to change. That's why, to make systems better, we must start by mapping culture. It's hard to see, but it's not invisible. If we look beneath the surface, we see that like art, music and all the webs we weave, culture is a reflection of ourselves and our unquenchable thirst for connection.

CHAPTER 4

Culture

*"The power of authoritative knowledge is
not that it is correct but that it counts."*
– BRIGITTE JORDAN

They stride into the arena wearing the maize and blue. They
are tall, strong, fast, and confident they will conquer the
world. It wasn't easy getting here, but after countless hours of
practice, weight training, and gut-busting cardio workouts,
they have arrived. The price is high. It costs thousands of
dollars a year to play at this level, but without access to the
best coaches, facilities, and technologies, you might as well
just go home.

It's six-thirty in the morning in January, and as I watch our
fourteen year old daughter's volleyball team make their way
to the court, my feelings are mixed. I'm not happy about
waking up at five o'clock on a Saturday to drive for an hour
through the snow. A few years ago, I'd have laughed at this
elite sports scene. Now I'm a part of it. Claire is staying fit,
making friends, building self-confidence, learning teamwork.

Still, it's over the top. Our club makes me uneasy. What bothers me most is the uniforms. They are beautiful. Since our club is run by the *University of Michigan*, our girls are decked out in blue and gold. While a lot of teams satisfice with cotton t-shirts, we have personalized, lightweight, wicking *Nike* jerseys with matching shorts, warm ups, and backpacks. As our girls prepare to play, I can't help feeling we're on the wrong side of the tracks. And sure enough, we are crushed by the t-shirt team, just like in the movies. Later, after a day of losses, I tell Claire not to worry, it's the first tournament of a six-month season, the team will get better.

Of course, it was all downhill from there. Our coach was a hard-ass all season. One girl was berated for not hitting hard enough. Later it turned out her finger was broken. Claire was told she couldn't take a break even though she felt sick. Soon after she was vomiting into a bucket. The girls were taught how to trick the referee. They were instructed to lie. The coach invited them to voice complaints. Claire did so and found herself benched. The parents weren't any better. Our alpha mom reduced other moms to tears, taunted the opposing teams, and paid for weekly private lessons with the coach. This looked like pay-to-play corruption to us, but several of the parents said that's simply how you play the game.

The next year we switched clubs. The new one was a little less expensive and a whole lot better. When the coach told the girls it was okay to miss practice for homework, since education is more important than volleyball, he actually meant it. When we lose a game, you won't hear a word from our alpha mom. We don't have one. The girls practice in an old warehouse, no windows, flickering lights. It's nothing fancy. Neither are the uniforms. And that's the way we like it. We found our fit.

Cultural Fit

In the 1990s, as co-owner and CEO of a consulting practice, I hired and managed several dozen employees. Mostly we got it right, but once in a while we hired someone who didn't fit. The consequence of a cultural mismatch is often compared to an immune system response. It's not a bad analogy. The first symptom is inflammation. This pain is followed by isolation of the foreign body. But in organizations, there's no need to destroy the antigen. Few people endure outsider status for long. They quit. At the time I thought there was something wrong with those people. My enculturation was complete. Now I know it simply wasn't a good fit.

As a consultant for two decades, I've been a tourist in all sorts of cultures. I've worked with startups, Fortune 500 companies, nonprofits, Ivy League colleges, and Federal Government agencies in multiple countries. My clients have included folks from marketing, support, human resources, engineering, and design. Being exposed to diverse ways of knowing and doing is one of the best parts of my work. But my interest runs deeper than cultural tourism. Over the years, I've realized that understanding culture is central to what I do.

First, as an information architect, I must understand the culture of users. When I run a "usability test," evaluating the system is only half my aim. I also hope to uncover the beliefs, values, and behaviors of the people who use the system. Before imposing my own theories, I want to see how they define their world. What can we learn from their use of language and the way they sort concepts into categories? Which sources of information and authority do they trust? What is the meaning behind their behavior? For years, I've used lightweight forms of design ethnography as part of my user research practice. It's helped me to better understand and design for oncologists, middle school children, university faculty, bargain hunters, and network engineers. And, as the systems we design only grow more rooted in culture, I'm convinced we must dig deeper into ethnography.

Second, as an outside consultant, I must understand the culture of the organizations for which I work. Today's systems aren't only integral to the lives of users, but they are progressively part of the way we do business. To improve user experience, it may be necessary to change the org chart, metrics, incentives, processes, rules, and relationships. Connections and consequences run all the way from code to culture. Software that doesn't work "the way we work" will fail like an employee who doesn't fit. So we must also study and design for stakeholders. In my research, I always interview a mix of executives and employees about roles, responsibilities, vision, and goals. And I've learned that if I don't ask the right questions in the right way, or if I don't listen carefully and read between the lines, I may mistake the surface for substance and invent a design that won't fit.

Figure 4-1. We must design for a bi-cultural fit.

In short, the right design is one that fits the company and its customers. A mismatch on either side results in fatal error. We must use ethnography with our users and stakeholders to search for a *bi-cultural* fit. This is tricky since culture is mostly invisible. That's why we should start with a map.

Mapping Culture

Edgar Schein, professor emeritus at MIT and the father of the study of corporate culture, offers a useful definition.

> Culture is a pattern of shared tacit assumptions that was learned by a group as it solved its problems of external adaptation and internal integration, that has worked well enough to be considered valid and to be taught to new members as the correct way to perceive, think, and feel in relation to those problems.[1]

Culture is a powerful, often unconscious set of forces that shape both our individual and collective behavior. In an organization, culture is reflected in "the way we do things here." It influences goals, governance, strategy, planning, hiring, metrics, management, status, and rewards.

And culture is an artifact of history. Organizational culture is rooted in the values of the entrepreneur. In the early days, as leaders struggle to build the business, the beliefs and behaviors that lead to success are internalized. Eventually they become taken for granted, invisible, and non-negotiable.

At this point, it's difficult to decipher the culture without a compass or map. Fortunately, Edgar Schein's model offers the orientation we need. We can use his *Three Levels of Culture* to ask questions about any institution.

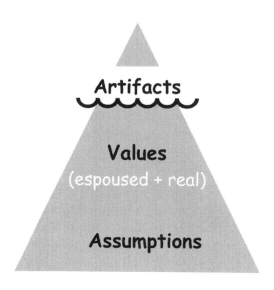

Figure 4-2. Three levels of culture.

First, what will a visitor see, hear, and feel? Artifacts include architecture, interior design and layout, technology, process, work style, social interactions, and meetings. Who's the boss? How can you tell? Is there music? Are people talking? What do they wear? Where do they sit? When do they eat? What makes 'em smile? Artifacts are easy to see but hard to decode. The art on the wall is visible but what does it mean? Why's it there? Artifacts aren't answers, but they raise good questions.

Second, what are the mission, vision, and values? How about goals, strategy, brand? Websites, annual reports, and those colorful posters so artfully framed in the lobby offer a place to start, but interviews with insiders are the only way to the truth. Espoused values are hard to miss yet often inconsistent with behavior, which is why we need "informants" to help us see what's really going on. If teamwork is a core value, why are individuals so competitive? If the organization is user-centered, why doesn't anyone talk to users? It's vital to listen carefully as insiders may not know or be willing to tell the truth. Dissonance and its justifications serve as keys to the invisible culture. Entry is earned by paying attention.

Third, what are the tacit beliefs that are taken for granted and non-negotiable? Level three is all about history. What were the ways of the founders that led to success? Are they still valid or holding us back? When we fail to seize the future, it's often because we're blinded to the present by the radiance of our past success. Assumptions are the bedrock of culture. They are hidden and resistant to change. As organizations grow, technologies advance, and markets evolve, friction between old assumptions and new realities is inevitable, but people don't question what they can't see. This is where an advisor can help. Only insiders can effect cultural change, but it often takes an outsider to sketch the map.

Subcultures

No culture is an island. To understand any culture, we must study its context. For example, Ed Schein notes that "in some organizations the subcultures are as strong or stronger than the overall organizational culture."[2] It may be useful to think of them as "co-cultures" to avoid false assumptions about influence and power. To succeed we must employ multiple levels of analysis and seek leverage in the layer that counts.

A few years ago, I was asked to evaluate site search for one of the world's largest technology firms. The problems were painfully obvious. Customer satisfaction surveys showed findability to be the #1 complaint. Search analytics data revealed a zero click-through rate of forty-eight percent. In nearly half of all queries, users failed to click on a single result. And in my user research, I saw people fail to find basic content, over and over again. One customer summed up the search results interface by stating "There's a lot of garbage here. And the filters are all gobbledygook."

I was excited by this opportunity to make search better, but I soon hit a roadblock. As I led stakeholder interviews, a pattern emerged. The folks in Support were eager to fix site search, but those in Marketing weren't very interested. Most of them were too polite to say it straight, but it wasn't hard to read between the lines. They were enthusiastic about search engine optimization as it offered new customers and easy metrics, but site search didn't fit their sense of mission. They didn't study it in business school. This was a major problem, as Marketing owned the website and held all the money and power.

So, I worked with my clients in Support to craft a message that would resonate with the people in Marketing. We used data, told stories, and invoked experts. Here's an excerpt.

> Gerry McGovern argues that "Support is the new Marketing." This hints at the emerging tendency of customers to evaluate a company's online support as part of the pre-purchase process. Our prospective customers and partners are smart. They know that Support is a vital component of the total cost of ownership. If they can't find what they need quickly, they lose time and business. Also, we can help users become aware of related products and services while seeking support. If done in a user-centered manner, this cross-sell and up-sell can be a win-win-win for us, our partners, and our customers…Mark Hurst says "the experience is the brand." He's acknowledging the tectonic shift from push to pull that's driven by the Internet. While names, logos, prices, packaging, and product quality are all still contributors to the brand, people's perceptions are increasingly shaped by their experiences with the website. When customers can't find what they need, the brand suffers. In an era of user-centered design, where expectations are shaped by positive experiences with consumer sites from Amazon to Zappos, it's clear that the sad state of site search is damaging and merits further attention and investment.

We asked customers to solve problems using the site, and captured video footage so stakeholders could see, feel, and share their frustration. We also appealed to the original source of the organization's success, the culture of Engineering, noting the potential of a slow, broken search system to embarrass a technology firm known for its software and hardware. Finally, we delivered a blueprint and a roadmap. We inspired confidence that these difficult problems could be solved. And it worked. We spoke the language of their culture, and they listened. Together we made search better.

Of course, when it comes to co-cultures, there are some things you just can't fix. I saw this first-hand while working with DaimlerChrylser soon after the 1998 merger. We were hired to build an information architecture strategy for a unified corporate portal. By integrating several American and German intranets into a single source of truth, executives hoped to bring the cultures together. While this seemed unrealistic, we were willing to give it a go. But the more we learned, the less we believed in the mission. In stakeholder interviews, the absence of trust was palpable.

This was a culture clash of epic proportions. On the surface, friction was caused by different wage structures, org charts, values, and brands. But at a deeper level, conflict was driven by differences in national culture. The entrepreneurial frontier spirit and individualism of the Americans did not fit with the methodical, risk-averse, team-oriented, bureaucratic culture of the Germans. At the time, we didn't understand all the forces at work, but we knew the unified portal would never happen. Of course, that was the least of their worries. Eventually the failed merger resulted in a market loss of over $30 billion. Nowadays people agree it didn't fail because the strategy was unsound. It's a deal that was killed by culture.

This story serves as a reminder that corporate culture is rooted in the national culture in which an organization operates. This brings us to the work of Geert Hofstede, a pioneer of cross-cultural research, who offers us an onion as a metaphor for understanding the cultures of countries.[3]

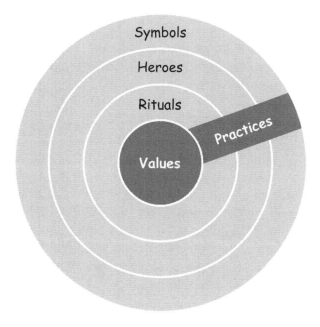

Figure 4-3. The Cultural Onion.

Symbols are words, images, objects, and gestures with special meaning to those in the culture. Heroes are people, alive or dead, real or imaginary, who exhibit role model qualities. Rituals are activities that are technically superfluous but socially essential, like how we say please and thank you. All three can be seen as practices and are visible to the outside observer. The hidden core is formed by values, defined as "broad tendencies to prefer certain states of affairs over others."[4] Our feelings about good and evil, danger, beauty, and nature are values, and they're acquired in childhood. Practices come later. They are learned at school and work.

In a heroic effort to make the invisible visible, Geert Hofstede led a multi-national, multi-decade research program to study cultural differences. He concluded that six dimensions – *power distance, individualism, masculinity, uncertainty avoidance, pragmatism, and indulgence* – offer insight into what makes us tick differently. Let's take a look by comparing two countries.

Power distance describes the degree to which members of society accept and expect the unequal distribution of power. In the United States where "all men are created equal," the score is low relative to China where formal authority, hierarchy, and inequality require no justification. As inequality continues to rise in the U.S. we can expect cultural resistance.

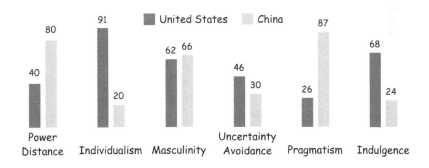

Figure 4-4. Hofstede's Cultural Dimensions.

Individualism measures interdependence among members. The U.S. is the most individualist society in the world. People are expected to look after themselves and their direct family. In contrast, China is collectivist with an emphasis less on "I" than "we." People belong to "in-groups" that take care of them in return for loyalty and preferential treatment.

Masculine cultures are driven by competition, assertiveness, and material success, whereas feminine societies like Sweden and Norway value cooperation, modesty, caring for the weak, and quality of life. Both the U.S. and China are masculine. In masculine societies, homosexuality is seen as a threat, and the label of this dimension is politically incorrect.

In an uncertainty avoidance culture like Japan, plans and rituals are used to manage risk, ambiguity, and fear of the unknown future. The U.S. and China score low. Both are open to new ideas, practices, and technologies.

Pragmatism is about how we relate to our inability to explain the world. In the normative U.S. people seek absolute Truth in science, religion, and politics, and we evaluate performance using simple, short-term metrics. In pragmatic China, the truth depends on context, traditions can be changed, thriftiness is admirable, and the long term is really what counts.

Indulgence measures the degree to which people control their desires. In a restrained society such as China, people adhere to strict social norms, tend to be cynical, and hold a low view of leisure. In the indulgent U.S. we're fairly free to gratify natural drives by enjoying life and having fun.

Geert Hofstede argues these values are built atop national paradigms – *China (family), Germany (order), Britain (systems), U.S. (markets)* – and that together they interact to shape the unique culture of each country. Also, he asks us to consider relationships between cultures at multiple levels.

> National value systems should be considered given facts, as hard as a country's geographical position or its weather. Layers of culture acquired later in life tend to be more changeable. This is the case, in particular, for organizational cultures, which the organization's members joined as adults. It doesn't mean that changing organizational culture is easy, but at least it is feasible.[5]

Our beliefs and behaviors emerge from interactions between the cultures of nations, organizations, communities, families; and the forces of individual personality and human nature. It's not worth trying to draw clear boundaries. Instead, we should aim for a rough map of the relevant co-cultures and contexts in which they exist. A deep dive into culture reveals "turtles all the way down," but that's no reason to give up. Between perfect vision and total blindness lies all the truth we know.

Ways of Knowing

Brigitte Jordan, the legendary corporate anthropologist and beloved godmother of design ethnography, made a mark early in her career with a brilliant series of cross-cultural studies of childbirth. In one, conducted in a U.S. city hospital in the 1980s, she used video, medical records, and postpartum interviews to explore and describe the culture of obstetrics.

> The people present in the labor room with the woman are her husband and a nurse...The husband appears intimidated...The nurse is in a delicate position...she needs to assess the woman's state within a small range of error in order to be able to call the physician in time for the crucial stages of delivery that require his presence, but not so early as to waste his valuable time...she is very much preoccupied with the electronic fetal monitor (EFM)...even though it has never been shown that routine EFM treatment improves birth outcome...The woman is not allowed to push. Every effort is made to keep her from giving in to the overpowering impulse to bear down. She is asked to suppress the urge long enough for the physician to come in and pronounce her ready. The physician is paged several times but does not appear...The physician finally arrives, together with a male medical student. He examines the woman and declares she is ready to push. The staff prepare her for delivery...The child is delivered by the medical student who announces it's a boy...Finally, several minutes after the baby is born, he is given to his mother to hold. [6]

In the half hour before the baby is born, the woman "knows she has to push and says so clearly." The nurse largely ignores the woman's body and voice but repeatedly checks the EFM (*19 times in 5 minutes*). When the doctor enters the room, he doesn't talk to the woman, and after making his decision, he says "she can push" and the nurse relays the message.

Throughout the labor, participants work hard to maintain the definition of the situation as one where the woman's knowledge counts for nothing. They all know she "cannot" push until the doctor gives the official go-ahead. Within this particular knowledge system, it is believed that only the doctor can tell when a woman is ready to push – information he gains from checking the dilation of the cervix during a vaginal examination. This fiction is maintained collaboratively, by the woman herself, her husband, the nurse, the medical student – in the face of the fact that anybody who cares to look or listen can see that this woman's body is ready to push the baby out…However, what the woman knows and displays, by virtue of her bodily experience, has no status.

In short, the woman is treated as an object, and the doctor is in charge of the facts. Jordan uses this powerful ethnography to illustrate the concept of "authoritative knowledge."

Within any social situation a multitude of ways of knowing exist, but some carry more weight than others. Some kinds of knowledge become discredited and devalued, while others become socially sanctioned, consequential, even "official," and are accepted as grounds for legitimate inference and action…The legitimation of one way of knowing as authoritative devalues, often totally dismisses, all other ways of knowing…The constitution of authoritative knowledge is an ongoing social process that both builds and reflects power relationships within a community of practice…The power of authoritative knowledge is not that it is correct but that it counts.

To be fair, we may rely on hierarchical decision-making for good reason, but authoritative knowledge is driven by both efficacy and power. So it's naïve to inquire which way is better. Better for whom? Better in which contexts? Better for what purposes? These are the questions we must ask.

Not so long ago, our ways of knowing were different. Before the printing press, we relied heavily upon personal experience and our senses, using evidence and *induction* to find the truth. In time, we extended our senses with instruments and formalized trial-and-error as the scientific method. We added to our empirical ways with *deduction*, using reason and logic to mathematically prove the truth. To absorb *second-hand knowledge*, we had to do it in person. Cultural wisdom was embodied in rituals, habits, laws, and myths. Power, authority, and trust were centered in the community.

Today most knowledge is second-hand, and we don't even know where it comes from. Access to massive amounts of conflicting information from myriad sources creates filter failure. We don't know what to believe. So we fall back on simple ways of knowing. We trust experts and those in authority. We follow doctor's orders. Or we reject expertise completely. Like U.S. senator James Inhofe, we know global warming is a hoax, because it's cold outside. Of course, we're not forced to a single extreme. We may allow for many inputs, and then use *intuition* to feel our way to the truth.

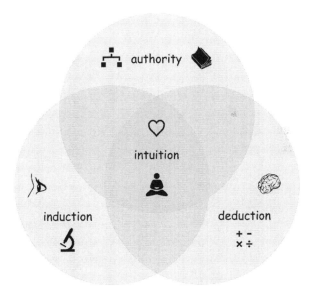

Figure 4-5. Ways of knowing.

We do this often in our personal lives, but it's tricky to pull off in business. It's hard to ask others to "trust my gut" so we routinely manufacture evidence. Experts are hired to validate the course of action. User studies are designed to approve the interface. Metrics are defined to back the plan. It's amazing how much is done in support of what we already know.

Within a culture, the idiosyncrasy of authoritative information is mostly invisible. Insiders rarely question their institutional ways of knowing. As a consultant, I've had clients who place too much faith in my expertise, and others who don't trust enough. Some use "usability tests" as the sole source of truth. Others track conversions as the way to know what's right. And an awful lot of folks simply believe the boss knows best.

As an outsider, it's my role to ask the questions that never get asked, but when I begin I have no idea what they are or where to find them. So I use a multi-method research process that affords breadth and depth. I wallow in data of all sorts and talk to people from all walks. While I begin with observation and analysis, I'm aiming for insight and synthesis. Towards this end, I find lightweight forms of ethnography to be great tools for digging into the cultures of users and stakeholders.

Design Ethnography

Unsurprisingly, Clifford Geertz, the eminent pioneer of symbolic anthropology, defines culture metaphorically.

> Believing, with Max Weber, that man is an animal suspended in webs of significance he himself has spun, I take culture to be those webs, and the analysis of it to be not an experimental science in search of law but an interpretive one in search of meaning.[7]

Ethnography is how we discover and describe this meaning, and Geertz argues it isn't defined by a methodology but by a particular way of knowing. "What defines it is the kind of intellectual effort it is: an elaborate venture in, to borrow a notion from Gilbert Ryle, thick description."[8]

A thin description of the superficial behavior that's easily accessible via observation misses the point. In the contraction of an eyelid lies the vast distance between an involuntary twitch and a conspiratorial wink. The ethnographer needs to understand the meaning behind the behavior.

In *The Ethnographic Interview*, James Spradley offers a thick description of the art of thick description. He sees words as keys to culture, noting "language is more than a means of communication about reality: it is a tool for constructing reality."[9] He enjoins ethnographers to pay attention to the words we hear and use. For instance, the people we study and interview are *informants*, not subjects, respondents, or actors.

> Ethnographers adopt a particular stance toward people with whom they work. By word and action, in subtle ways and direct statements, they say, "I want to understand the world from your point of view. I want to know what you know in the way you know it. I want to understand the meaning of your experience, to walk in your shoes, to feel things as you feel them, to explain things as you explain them. Will you become my teacher and help me understand?"[10]

We must be careful how we ask questions. Spradley recounts his experiences studying the "homeless men" who turned out to be "tramps" noting that if you ask "where do you live?" they answer "I have no home." They use *translation competence* or "the ability to translate the meanings of one culture into a form that is appropriate to another culture."[11] They tell you what they think you want to hear in your language. But if you admit ignorance and ask descriptive questions (*e.g., Tell me about a day in your life. Where do you sleep? Where do you eat? What do you do?*) you may learn about "making a flop" and realize that they aren't homeless after all.

I discovered that making a flop was such a rich phrase that I scarcely scratched the surface of its meaning. My informants identified more than a hundred different categories of flops. They had strategies for locating flops, for protecting themselves from the weather and intruders in flops. Making a flop defined their friendship patterns and even their police record…I realized that, in some ways, a flop was like a home to a tramp, but I did not merely translate the one term into the other for my ethnography. Instead I worked to elucidate the full meaning of this concept, to describe their culture in its own terms.[12]

Ethnography is tricky since we aim to discover from our informants not just the answers but the questions as well. It's all too easy to impose our assumptions on their culture. In observations and interviews, we should aim for what Zen Buddhists call "beginner's mind" – an attitude of openness, awareness, and curiosity without beliefs or expectations. If we study high school students, for instance, instead of starting with specific questions about academics or athletics, we might say "If I sat at your table at lunch, what sorts of things might I hear?" This invites our informants to tell us about topics that are important to them in their own language.

Of course, perfect openness is neither possible nor desirable. As ethnographers, we seek insights to advance our goals. Spradley's list of universal cultural themes serves as a good place to start. He suggests we look for social conflict, cultural contradictions, informal techniques of control (*e.g., gossip, rewards*), strategies for dealing with strangers, and ways of acquiring and maintaining status. Similarly, Hofstede offers an interview checklist, but his is aimed at corporate culture.

Symbols: What are the special terms that only insiders understand?

Heroes: What kinds of people advance quickly in their careers here? Whom do you consider as particularly meaningful persons for this organization?

Rituals: In what periodic meetings do you participate? How do people behave during those meetings? Which events are celebrated in this organization?

Values: What things do people like to see happening here? What is the biggest mistake one can make? What work problems can keep you awake at night? [13]

And Edgar Schein tells us to "decipher the reward-and-status system. What kind of behavior is expected, and how do you know when you are doing the right or wrong thing?"[14] While pay increases and promotions do matter, less obvious forms of social currency may also be powerful.

Finally, as information architects, we may ask about the use of systems and services. What tools do you use, and why? Can you show me how you achieve that goal? What happens when this tool doesn't work? Where you do go to find answers? How do you know who to trust? It appears we could ask questions all day, but as Spradley reminds us, we're less interested in surface-level specifics than deep structure.

Cultural knowledge is more than random bits of information; [it] is organized into categories, all of which are systematically related to the entire culture.[15]

Culture is a system of symbols and relationships. Using domain analysis and taxonomy construction, ethnographers make maps that show how people have organized their knowledge. The first step is to describe the domain by identifying categories, connections, and boundaries.

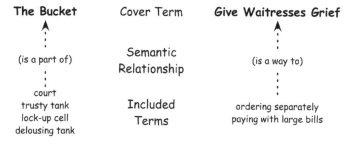

The Bucket	Cover Term	Give Waitresses Grief
▲		▲
(is a part of)	Semantic Relationship	(is a way to)
court trusty tank lock-up cell delousing tank	Included Terms	ordering separately paying with large bills

Figure 4-6. Elements in a domain.[16]

This domain analysis builds towards taxonomy construction and the mapping of attributes and semantic relationships.

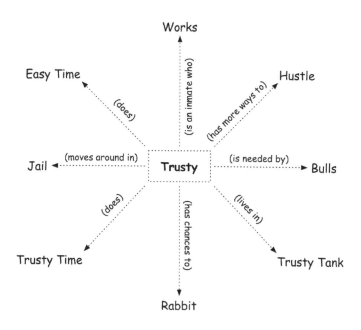

Figure 4-7. Attributes and semantic relationships.[17]

The folk taxonomy or "set of categories organized on the basis of a single semantic relationship" is the core. Analysis may reveal the attributes and relationships for each folk term.

Here, ethnography and information architecture are indistinguishable. Taxonomies are boundary objects used in many ways by many communities. But our practices diverge in their goals. An ethnographer's work concludes with a "thick description" and the understanding of a culture, while the information architect aims to create or change a system.

So our approach to ethnography differs from that of an anthropologist. We have less time for field work, but that's mitigated by more directed goals. Since we're focused on interactions with systems and services, in addition to asking questions, we use sketches and prototypes to probe for possibility. We're interested in *what is* and *what if* as well.

Levers of Change

Early in my career, I designed some fancy information architectures that were never built, and others that failed to stand the test of time. I had a freshly minted degree in library science and knew all sorts of ways to structure and organize information, but I didn't realize the value of the right fit. My designs were technically elegant but culturally clumsy. I paid scant attention to silos, subcultures, and reward-and-status systems. My clients paid the price. On the bright side, they learned valuable lessons about change. In *The Fifth Discipline*, Peter Senge argues for systems thinking as the basis for learning organizations, and defines eleven laws, including:

The cure can be worse than the disease.

The harder you push, the harder the system pushes back.

The easy way out usually leads back in.[18]

One of the most useful things I've learned in twenty years of consulting is that change is surprisingly difficult. Most interventions fail to stick. Organizations get all jazzed up about *the way things could be* only to revert to *the way things are.*

Figure 4-8. The power of organizational inertia.

This is discouraging, but lasting change is possible if we work to understand the source of inertia. As Peter Senge explains "Resistance is a response by the system, trying to maintain an implicit system goal. Until this goal is recognized, the change effort is doomed to failure."[19] Senge also offers a word of encouragement. "Small changes can produce big results, but the areas of highest leverage are often the least obvious."[20]

His insights capture my experience as an information architect precisely. In recent years, I've learned to *search for a fit* and to *look for the levers.* I aim to align my design with culture, and to the extent that a cultural shift is desirable, I look for sources of power while cultivating my own humility. My approach to intervention is inspired by the wisdom of Edgar Schein.

> Culture is deep. If you treat it as a superficial phenomenon, if you assume that you can manipulate it and change it at will, you are sure to fail.[21]

Schein warns us to "never start with the idea of changing a culture,"[22] but to begin with business goals and enlist culture as an ally when possible.

Since culture is very difficult to change, focus most of your energy on identifying the assumptions that can help you. Try to see your culture as a positive force to be used, rather than a constraint to be overcome.[23]

To identify opportunities for *cultural jujitsu*, a multi-level approach is most useful. If our design invites resistance from the corporate culture, for instance, perhaps we can look to an organizational subculture or the national culture or human nature for support. Also, rather than limit ourselves to a single tactic, we must embrace multiple *ways of changing*.

Information   Architecture   Behavior   Leadership   Synthesis

Figure 4-9. Multiple ways of changing.

Often, our first tactic for making change is *information*. To improve diets, we tell kids about the links between donuts, soda, obesity, and diabetes. To improve efficiency, we inform staff about new procedures or values. These educational interventions draw upon the power of authoritative information to change minds and behavior. While this tactic works well sometimes, it's easily thwarted by established habits and assumptions. People tend to deny data that proves inconvenient truths unless the driving forces (*burning platform, external threat, positive vision*) are greater than the restraining forces (*self-justification, fear of change, cultural inertia*).

To offset defensiveness, we may need to guide folks through a U-shaped process that makes room for learning through unlearning. By observing the system and mapping the whole, we unfreeze beliefs and open minds. We help folks understand the context and consequences of their actions.

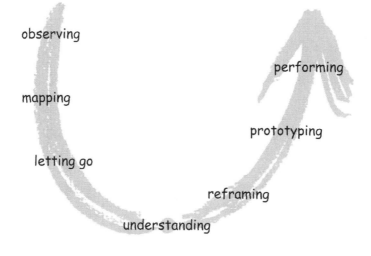

observing

performing

mapping

prototyping

letting go

reframing

understanding

Figure 4-10. U-shaped learning.

As Otto Scharmer, a leading proponent of *Theory U*, explains:

> The journey from ego-system to eco-system awareness or from "me" to "we" has three dimensions: (1) better relating to others; (2) better relating to the whole system; (3) better relating to oneself. These three dimensions require participants to explore the edges of the system and the self.[24]

This is why ethnography is so vital to design. Personal interaction with users leads to insight and empathy. When we see customers struggling and suffering, we're motivated to improve our systems. Often, to create change, information isn't enough. People need to care about the outcome.

Relative to information, *architecture* is a less direct but more persuasive path to change. Of course, the two tactics usually work best when paired. For instance, asking designers and engineers to collaborate may have a limited effect, unless we also co-locate their desks. As Winston Churchill famously remarked "We shape our buildings; thereafter they shape us."

In *Nudge*, Richard Thaler and Cass Sunstein define a "choice architect" as a person responsible for "organizing the context in which people make decisions."[25] They note that by rearranging a school cafeteria, it's possible to increase or decrease the consumption of many food items by as much as 25 percent.[26] Of course the context need not be physical. In one study, forty thousand people were asked "Do you intend to buy a new car in the next six months?" The act of asking the question increased purchase rates by 35 percent.[27] In another study, changing a retirement plan from opt-in to opt-out bumped up long-term enrollment from 65 to 98 percent.[28]

The practice of information architecture has been all about nudging users by organizing context. We design taxonomies, order search results, and define all sorts of defaults to shape behavior by priming. Now, if we hope to create deep, enduring change, we must turn our rhetoric on ourselves. This is the hidden need Dave Gray has met with culture mapping.

> In most large-scale organizational change projects, culture is the "elephant in the room." It is not only undiscussed, it is undiscussable, at least in any serious, meaningful way. And yet it is the biggest threat to any major change.[29]

To understand and change a culture, you must make the invisible visible, so Dave offers us a "Culture Map," inspired by the work of Ed Schein, that asks a series of questions.

Evidence. How do we behave? What is observable (*the language we use, the spaces we work in, how we collaborate, compete, create, control*)?

Levers. What are the rules of the game that drive behavior (*who controls what, decisions, resource allocation, rewards, workspace design*)?

Values. What are the stated values (*public statements*)? How about the acted values (*inferred from evidence, demonstrated by behavior*)?

Assumptions. Based on acted values. Why do we believe they will help us succeed (*or confer competitive advantage in our marketplace*)?

These questions are designed to help us reveal and map the structure of a culture, since the first step towards change is awareness of the architecture that already exists.

A third means of change is direct intervention in the routine, unconscious *behavior* patterns we call habits. In *The Power of Habit*, Charles Duhigg explores the science of habit formation and explains how to lose weight, achieve goals, and be more productive by hacking habits. He argues that "keystone habits" like exercise, diet, and family dinners can be fashioned into levers of change and used to start a chain reaction.

> When you learn to force yourself to go to the gym or start your homework or eat a salad instead of a hamburger, part of what's happening is that you're changing how you think. People get better at regulating their impulses. They learn how to distract themselves from temptations. And once you've got into that willpower groove, your brain is practiced at helping you focus on a goal.[30]

We need not change our habits all at once. In fact, it's best to start small. As B.J. Fogg, the inventor of *Tiny Habits*, explains:

> The number one mistake people make is not going tiny enough. If you're trying to make a change in your life, you need to add something to your routine that is smaller than small, smaller than tiny, something minuscule, that takes almost no effort or time. This eliminates not only running as a new habit, but also running around the block or running down the driveway. Just put on your running shoes. That's it. Put them on in the morning every day for five days. You're done. Push-ups? You don't do 10 push-ups. You do one. Flossing? You don't floss your teeth. You floss one tooth.[31]

At first this sounds absurd. One tooth? Seriously? But there's a method to Fogg's madness. He asks people to practice their tiny habits in a particular way. A habit must require little effort, take less than 30 seconds, and be done at least once a day. The habit must be preceded by an anchor, an existing habit or event that triggers the new behavior. And the tiny habit must be followed by a reward or self-celebration. So, for instance, you may decide that "After I brush my teeth, I'll floss one tooth, then shout Victory!"

Anchor   *triggers*   Tiny Habit   *rewarded by*   Celebration

Figure 4-11. The architecture of tiny habits.

Tiny habits are the building blocks of behavior. Fogg's method makes the architecture of behavior visible, so we can see how to change what we do. After working with 10,000 people, he has proven that if you start small and take it one step at a time, you'll see that tiny habits really add up.

Habits can be practiced not only by individuals but by teams as well, as this anecdote by Clay Shirky reveals.

> Every now and again, I see a business doing something so sensible and so radical at the same time that I realize I'm seeing a little piece of the future. I had that feeling last week, after visiting my friend Scott Heiferman at Meetup. On my way out after a meeting, Scott pulled me into a room by the elevators, where a couple of product people were watching a live webcam feed of someone using Meetup. Said user was having a hard time figuring out a new feature, and the product people, riveted, were taking notes. It was the simplest setup I'd ever seen for user feedback, and I asked Scott how often they did that sort of thing. "Every day" came the reply.[32]

In most businesses, user research is sporadic, and only a few specialists participate in direct observation. But it's not very difficult or expensive to create a setup that lets people who build systems watch people use those systems on a routine basis. Imagine how much better our systems and services might be if more teams made user research a regular habit.

Of course, cultural change must come from the top, but even with strong *leadership*, it's hard to move the needle. Charles Duhigg tells the story of Paul O'Neil who set out to change the keystone habits of worker safety at Alcoa. In his first speech as CEO, he surprised his audience of investors and analysts.

> I want to talk to you about worker safety. Every year, numerous Alcoa workers are injured so badly they miss a day of work. Our safety record is better than the general American workforce, especially considering that our employees work with metals that are 1500 degrees and machines that can rip a man's arm off. But it's not good enough. I intend to make Alcoa the safest company in America. I intend to go for zero injuries.[33]

The audience was confused. Usually, new CEOs explained how they would lower costs, avoid taxes, and boost profits, but O'Neil talked only about safety. After the speech, financial advisors told clients to dump the stock. And initially, employees didn't get on board either. They had all learned not to trust the words of executives. Then, six months into his tenure, O'Neil got a call in the middle of the night. A new hire had been killed while repairing a machine. The next day, after due diligence, O'Neil gathered all the plant executives and Alcoa's top officers, and he gave another speech.

> We killed this man. It's my failure of leadership. I caused his death. And it's the failure of all of you in the chain of command. [34]

O'Neil assumed responsibility for the incident and presented a plan to make sure it never happened again. He invited people of all ranks to contact him directly about safety, and when they did, he made sure the problems got fixed. Employees began to believe in the mission, and the culture steadily transformed. Soon Alcoa became the safest company in

America. And its profits and market capitalization hit record highs. Safety turned out to be a keystone habit that started a chain reaction, but it took an act of leadership to write the story that made the people believe.

The folk singer and activist Pete Seeger is another leader who knew how to walk the talk. He didn't just sing in support of freedom. In 1955, when subpoenaed to testify before the *House Un-American Activities Committee*, Seeger refused to answer their questions and was cited for contempt and sentenced to a year in jail. And he didn't just preach environmentalism but lived it, as the blues guitarist Guy Davis recalls in a story.

> We were driving back from Amherst to an afternoon gig in Poughkeepsie. We had an hour to kill. We took a rest at this little walkway mall to take a nap, and we leaned our backs against a fountain. It was about ten feet in diameter with a brick wall. I closed my eyes and fell asleep. The next thing I know, I heard some splashing. I opened my eyes up, turned around, there's Pete with his pants rolled up in the water picking the garbage out of the fountain, and he's got these kids helping him, and I said to myself "this man is no hypocrite."[35]

There's a similar story about the *Ann Arbor District Library*. The director, Josie Parker, assumed leadership in the wake of a scandal. The former finance director had been found guilty of fraud. To regain the trust of the community, Josie set out to build "a culture of generosity." In time, her efforts became visible on all levels, from the forgiveness of fines to construction of new branch libraries which are among the most beautiful buildings in town. One day, during the holiday season, Josie was volunteering at a bookstore, wrapping gifts to raise money for charity. People had been generous that day, and the donation jar was filled with dollars and change. Suddenly a man grabbed the jar and ran for the door. Josie chased and tackled him, fracturing her leg in the process. The thief escaped empty-handed, and the story made national news with a headline of "the librarian who saved Christmas."

Each of these three leaders embodied their values and inspired people to tell their story. A compelling vision isn't enough. Actions and words must fit. We withhold belief in the absence of behavior. But since only a few may witness the original act, it must be sufficiently interesting to be shared widely. In short, to change a culture, you must change the story.

We've examined four *ways of changing* – information, architecture, behavior, leadership – while saving the best for last. Synthesis is how we combine these elements into a holistic plan. None of them stands alone. One way is the wrong way to change culture. To overcome resistance, we must engage on multiple fronts. Marc Rettig offers a model for parallel thinking which builds upon William Gibson's insight that "The future exists today. It's just unevenly distributed." Rettig tells us to identify the seeds around us that hold the promise of a better tomorrow.[36] If we show progress on multiple fronts by nurturing seeds into sprouts and helping people connect the dots, we can create momentum for change.

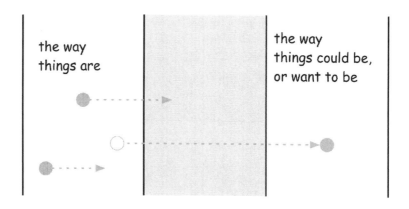

Figure 4-12. Marc Rettig's seeds and sprouts.

In the 1990s, researchers proved the efficacy of this sort of approach by applying the concept of "positive deviance" to the stubborn problem of malnutrition in Vietnam. First, they enlisted villagers to help identify unusually well-nourished children. Then, using ethnographic methods, they learned these families were collecting foods considered inappropriate for children (*sweet potato greens, shrimp, crab*). Also, contrary to cultural norms, these "positive deviants" were feeding their kids three to four times a day, and washing their hands before and after each meal. A nutrition program based on these insights was created, and it worked. In two years, malnutrition fell by 85 percent. As the researchers explain, the approach leads to success because it starts with locally grown seeds.

> Positive deviant behavior is an uncommon practice that confers advantage to the people who practice it compared with the rest of the community. Such behaviors are likely to be affordable, acceptable, and sustainable as they are already practiced by at risk people, they do not conflict with local culture, and they work. [37]

I'm reminded of a project for Hewlett-Packard in which we discovered an example of positive deviance. We were asked to redesign the information architecture of the @hp employee portal. The existing system was the end result of a centralized, top-down redesign that failed to meet the needs of employees. The plan was to fix it with a centralized, top-down redesign. During our research, we stumbled upon a brilliant annotated index. Built and maintained by and for the administrative staff of HP Labs, it boasted an organized, curated list of contacts, links, and instructions. It was an unofficial, under the radar, totally awesome guide for getting things done. We held it up as an example of the decentralized, bottom-up tools that employees should be encouraged to create in order to complement the top-down structures we'd been asked to design. Sadly, there wasn't much interest. In 2001, executives weren't marching the HP way. But the idea was solid. Small wins, like an annotated index, are the right place to start.

Alone, each small win stands a good chance of making it past the cultural immune system. Together, multiple small wins create a visible pattern of progress. V.S. Ramachandran explains that "Culture consists of massive collections of complex skills and knowledge which are transferred from person to person through two core mediums, language and imitation."[38] We can use this monkey see, monkey do proclivity to our advantage. Once people perceive a trend, they are infinitely more likely to adopt a new tool, process, belief, or value. Under certain conditions, after passing the proverbial tipping point, a culture can change shockingly fast.

So, culture is not an immovable object. If we use multiple *ways of changing* in concert, we may be able to move the needle. But we must be ready for curveballs, since people make complex systems even less predictable. For instance, five years ago, I went bald. I mean, it had been going on for a while, but one day I finished the job. My wife was out, so I showed our daughters first. "Claire, I have a surprise for you," I called, and our ten year old walked into the room. She then screamed, ran to the corner, curled into a fetal ball, and cried and cried and cried. I hugged her and told her it was okay, and then I cheered her up by suggesting we surprise her eight year old sister. But when we found Claudia, she surprised us instead, by staring me in the face and asking "what's the big surprise?"

When we change, some people totally freak out, while others don't notice or care, and it's only after you act that you understand who will do what. When Claire played for the maize and blue volleyball club, she and her teammates were unhappy with the way the coach ran practices. The girls were too scared to speak up, but I encouraged Claire to talk to her coach. The meeting went badly. The coach behaved defensively. She expected the players to accept her authority without question, but that's not the way we raise our girls, so the confrontation escalated, and the next game Claire was benched. It was a painful but useful lesson, and an illustration of Brigitte Jordan's insight that "the power of authoritative knowledge is not that it is correct but that it counts." Claire learned that in some cultures and contexts, it's best to keep your mouth shut, and escape as soon as you can.

As an information architect, I think about change on two levels. First, I identify opportunities for improvement that fit my client's culture. Once I've uncovered the problem and described a solution, these technical fixes become low-hanging fruit. Second, I explore innovative ways to improve the user experience that may be obstructed by the organizational culture. In this quest, I proceed very carefully. If I believe that change is possible, and if the cause is worth it, I may push hard. In the words of Brenda Laurel, I'll try "inserting new material into the cultural organism without activating its immune system."[39] Otherwise, I'll tactfully tell my client of the cultural constraints, and let them decide whether to act.

Experience teaches us that change is hard. Often we opt for the serenity of Paul McCartney's *Let It Be*. But once in a while we summon the courage to change the things we think we can. It doesn't always work out. Mostly we lack the wisdom to know the difference. Time and again, we don't know our own limits.

CHAPTER 5

Limits

*"In a single individual it can happen in a
millisecond. All it takes is a click in the
mind, a falling of scales from eyes, a new
way of seeing."*

– DONELLA MEADOWS

The end is near. The pain is great. I steal a glance at my wife
and our two beautiful daughters, but the moment is too much.
I fight back tears and watch my breath. I can't afford to lose
focus. Physically and emotionally, I'm devastated, but I've
come too far to collapse with the end in sight. So, I put one
foot in front of the other. I run past my limits and over the
line. A 7:12 pace for 26.2 miles. I've met my goal.

People said it couldn't be done. You're too old. It's your first
marathon. Go slow. Just aim to finish. But I would not yield.
My race began with research. I read all about the science of
endurance and nutrition. I changed my diet, learned to boost
my VO_2 max, and taught my brain to relax its thresholds. I
adopted the "run less, run faster" system for optimal

efficiency and minimal risk of injury.[1] I hoped to qualify for the *Boston Marathon* with no more pain than necessary. Still, two hour training runs open the door to doubt: push yourself, but not too hard, tendonitis is game over, all this suffering for naught. When I grew dispirited, I sustained myself with uplifting stories. In *Once a Runner* and *The Extra Mile*, I found the will to run on. As race day drew near, I studied a map, sketched a plan, and made a checklist.

The morning of the marathon was unseasonably cold, but I was prepared for surprises. I wore an extra shirt, gloves, two hats, and shorts, so I could shed layers over time. By the end, I was sweating, but not too much, and that's the lesson I learned. A marathon blends information, inspiration, and perspiration. What we read changes how we run. Grit is an essential ingredient, but the plan matters too. So does the goal. While it's fun to fix on a target, the pace isn't the point. Marathons, triathlons, and wilderness hiking quests are all part of a strategy to maintain a healthy mindbody. Each event is a tool for motivation. My race was a success before I ran it.

The architect Eliel Saarinen said "always design a thing by considering it in its next larger context: a chair in a room, a room in a house, a house in an environment, an environment in a city plan." I find this advice useful as an athlete, as a dad, and as an information architect.

In volleyball, we teach our girls that while it's fun to win, it's better to focus on teamwork, self-cultivation, and health. Ironically, this reframing leads to more wins. This holds true in design as well. All too often we hit the wall for want of a wide-angle lens. It may feel safe to focus on simple metrics, but it's not. Obstacles, opportunities, connections, and consequences are often revealed only by seeing the bigger picture. There are no closed systems. Everything is entangled from code to culture. That's why it's malpractice to design a product, service, or experience without considering strategy.

Organizational Strategy

Strategy is everyone's business. It's not just a corner office, ivory tower abstraction. It shapes belief and behavior at all levels. A strategy is a plan to achieve a goal. It's easy to have a bad plan, but is it even possible for an organization to have no plan? Of course, it's also easy to get hung up on semantics. Strategy and planning are often vilified by people with narrow definitions who fail to see that Agile is a strategy and Lean is a plan. These folks are blind to the next larger context.

In *Strategy Safari*, Henry Mintzberg uses the blind men and an elephant to kick off a tour of ten schools of thought within the discipline of strategic management. He shows each school is valid but incomplete. A strategy is a plan, but it's also a pattern, a position, and a perspective. No real strategy can be purely deliberate (*prescriptive*) or purely emergent (*descriptive*) since one prevents learning while the other prevents control.

> Strategy formation is judgmental designing, intuitive visioning, and emergent learning; it is about transformation as well as perpetuation; it must involve individual cognition and social interaction, cooperation as well as conflict; it has to involve analyzing before and programming after as well as negotiating during; and all of this must be in response to what can be a demanding environment. Just try to leave any of this out and watch what happens![2]

Strategy is a balancing act that's as difficult as it is unavoidable. While we tend to focus on corporate strategy, every team and individual is responsible for strategy. Of course we should know and align with the overall strategy. And we can serve as sensors by providing feedback during rollout. We might also offer insight before implementation, because strategy and tactics are intertwingled. If a plan is invalidated by reality, it's our responsibility to speak truth to power. At the same time, we must make plans to achieve our own goals. There is no such thing as a purely tactical unit.

When we pretend there's a boundary between strategy and tactics, we grant people permission not to think.

As information architects, it's vital we embrace this challenge given the intimate relationship between structure and strategy. Even in the industrial era, structure played a larger role than most folks realize. Alfred Chandler's *Strategy and Structure*, one of the most influential management books of the twentieth century, defined structure as follows.

> Structure can be defined as the design of organization through which the enterprise is administered. This design, whether formally or informally defined, has two aspects. It includes, first, the lines of authority and communication between the different administrative offices and officers and, second, the information and data that flow through these lines.[3]

Chandler described in painstaking detail the growth and administration of the largest corporations in the United States over a period of one hundred years, and his bestselling book gave rise to the familiar expression that "structure follows strategy." Sadly that wasn't his point. Thirty years later, in a new introduction, he set the record straight.

> Structure had as much impact on strategy as strategy had on structure. But as changes in strategy came chronologically before those of structure, and perhaps also because an editor at The MIT Press talked me into changing the title from *Structure and Strategy* to *Strategy and Structure*, the book appears to focus on how strategy defines structure rather than on how structure affects strategy. My goal from the start was to study the complex interconnections in a modern industrial enterprise between structure and strategy, and an ever-changing external environment.[4]

A lot has changed since the rise of the railroad and the multi-divisional corporation, but Alfred Chandler's insight is still relevant. In fact, the information age amplifies the importance of structure. Increasingly, we spend time and make decisions in "places made of information." These contexts that we create profoundly shape our beliefs and behaviors, but the links are hard to see, so we don't even know what we're missing.

Figure 5-1. Which comes first, strategy or structure?

Alfred Chandler saw "the existing structure of the enterprise shaped – usually holding back – changes in strategy." Over time, these firms failed to adapt and collapsed. This problem only grows worse. Half a century ago, the life expectancy of a Fortune 500 firm was 75 years. Now it's less than 15 years. The external environment is changing faster every day, and even our best organizations are failing to learn and adapt.

We can be more responsive but only by changing how we organize ourselves and manage information. We've hit the limits of reductionism. Silos, short-term metrics, and quick fixes are dead ends. We must read between the lines and dig beneath the surface to wrangle with structure. We must cultivate a new way of seeing. Insight isn't enough. To inspire action we must help others see what we see. We must practice what Pierre Wack, the French oil executive who pioneered scenario planning, called "the gentle art of re-perceiving."

I have found that getting to that management "Aha!" is the real challenge. It does not simply leap at you when you've presented all the alternatives, no matter how eloquent your expression or how beautifully drawn your charts. It happens when your message reaches the mental models of decision makers, obliges them to question their assumptions about how their business works, and leads them to change and reorganize their inner models of reality.[5]

To advance, we must slow down. Even the most brilliant strategy will fail without shared understanding and organizational support. Peter Drucker explained "culture eats strategy for breakfast" but we didn't really listen. We dove head first into user experience without capturing the hearts and minds of stakeholders. It worked for a while, sort of, but surface design is at its limits. We think we're making software, websites, and experiences, but we're not. We are agents of change within complex adaptive systems. Until we accept this mission, we will forever repeat our mistakes. It's time to go deep and shine a bright light, since we're all in this together.

Daylighting

Headwater streams are the origin of most rivers. They are the smallest parts of river networks but constitute the majority of river miles, and they provide vital ecosystem services.[6] They provide habitat for invertebrates, amphibians, fish, birds, insects, and plants. They also recharge their local groundwater systems, spread nutrients, remove pollution, reduce flooding, and sustain the health of downstream rivers, lakes, and bays.

Sadly, until recently, we didn't see their value, so we systematically buried headwater streams and used them as sewer pipes to transport waste. For decades, they were unnamed, unmapped, invisible. But, increased urban flooding and ecological awareness has led to a reversal. In more and more cities, from Kalamazoo, Michigan to Yonkers, New York, we have begun to map, name, and uncover buried streams.

Figure 5-2. Five things you won't see in a buried river.

This strategy can revitalize ecosystems and economies. Flood mitigation cuts insurance costs and raises property values, but cities also use *daylighting* as a catalyst for creating urban parks and greenways with bike trails and walking paths. Schools are weaving these habitats into biology and ecology curricula. And without the cover of darkness, polluters are being forced to clean up their mess. In cities of all sorts, people are growing healthier, happier, and more connected with nature.

Of course, revelation isn't just for rivers. Daylighting is also a metaphor for the mapmaking work we must do. We should use our categories and connections to reveal the hidden assumptions of culture; and sketch links and loops to explore the latent potential of systems; and realize mental models by drawing them outside our heads. By making the invisible visible, we can shift the context of vision and decision, but helping people to *see differently* is a skill we don't use enough. We focus on users but ignore stakeholders. We put experience before understanding. It's time to realize that daylighting isn't moonlighting. It's the most vital work that we do.

In 2005, only two years after its founding, Myspace was purchased by News Corporation for $580 million. For the next few years, it was the most popular social network in the world. But its new owners insisted on rapid monetization. Executives, under pressure to hit quarterly revenue targets, flooded the site with garish display ads. The strategy worked for a while until the whole system collapsed. Revenue rose to $605 million in 2008 but fell to $47 million by 2011 when Myspace was sold for $35 million. This was a costly lesson in the link between advertising and user experience. Today, Facebook limits ads to 5% of its newsfeed. Like Amazon, Google, and Twitter, they sacrifice quarterly results for user experience and brand loyalty. Most firms lack this discipline.

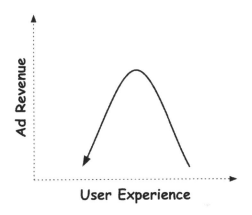

Figure 5-3. Advertising and the user experience.

Must they all learn the hard way? Or can we use stories and sketches to reveal what short-termism does to long-term health? To shift a mindset is not easy, but it's not impossible. Once in a while, we have an epiphany, when new information triggers a leap of understanding. But mostly, change is slow. It takes creativity, courage, and countless tiny steps.

I know people can change, because I've changed myself. A decade ago while in my early 30's I was diagnosed with high cholesterol. My doctor told me to change my habits or take medication. I did neither. Instead, I just got depressed. As a kid, soccer was my first love, but I was too old for that now. I was a workaholic dad with kids. I didn't have the time for exercise or the discipline to eat well. I was 35 lbs overweight and counting. The evidence suggested I'd continue adding weight as I endured middle age. I was unhappy, but what could I do? I had no strategy, no goal, and no sense of control.

I may not have escaped this state of learned helplessness if it wasn't for a giant plate of spaghetti and meatballs. My wife and I had invited a friend over for dinner. Andrew was a tall, muscular, twenty-something British rugby player. I'll never forget his look of shock when Susan handed him a plate. After a bit of gentle prodding, he confessed that he was surprised by its size. And, while Susan and I ate all our pasta, plus a few slices of garlic bread, to our chagrin Andrew ate only a third of his. Still, nothing changed, until a few months later when Susan stumbled upon an article that explained people eat less if they use smaller plates. The next day, our giant plates moved to the basement, and we began to eat dinner on dessert plates. For a while, we'd go back for seconds, but soon we simply ate less. It was our first tiny step on the road to health.

Figure 5-4. Context shapes behavior.

My sister-in-law inspired me to take the next step. She was in town for a half-marathon and cajoled me into a 5K. I did well for a couch potato, so she told me to try a ten-miler. I was scared of the distance but signed up for the race. The first weeks of training were hard. I felt I'd die in the heat. And my skin chafed horribly until I learned not to run in boxer shorts. But after a month I began to enjoy myself. I felt healthy in mind and body. I had reestablished my sense of control.

After that ten-miler, there was no turning back. I ran more half-marathons and a couple of marathons before shifting to triathlons for the long haul. I lost that 35 pounds. I sleep well and feel great. I've rediscovered the energy of that crazy kid who could play soccer all day long. But my journey hasn't only been physical. I've learned a lot about diet and exercise, but I've also become more aware of emotions, beliefs, and behaviors. I'm no longer held captive by the past. I've learned how to learn and change. And, for better or for worse, I've been granted the wisdom to question my culture.

Figure 5-5. Run, bike, swim.

At first it was little things. I quit soda and didn't miss it. So why did I drink it in the first place? Could it be the ubiquity and power of advertising? How much does it shape what we want? And how can we boost immunity? I read that stretching before exercise is harmful. It weakens muscles and invites injury. All my life I'd stretched before soccer games and races. Now everyone does it but me. I only stretch in the shower. At first my deviance was minor, but the distance only grew. In time I ran so far I left behind beefy portions of culture.

For instance, the more I read about nutrition, the more I questioned meat. My quest for health led me to study the ethics and environmental impact of our culture's carnivorism. I did a lot of reading and thinking, but it was *Eating Animals* by Jonathan Safran Foer that did the trick. My wife begged me not to read it, but I'm a red pill kinda guy. So I consumed the book and turned myself into a flexitarian, which means I annoy everyone. My wife is upset. She's a great cook, and I've cast a shadow over her recipes. Omnivores are unsettled. My choice invites them to question their own. And vegans are irate. How can I see the truth but continue to drink milk?

I'm convinced that normal factory farming practices are deeply immoral. The environmental impact is catastrophic, and the abuse of antibiotics and growth hormones is hazardous to human health. But it's the cruelty to animals that pushes me over the edge. My moral circle is a fuzzy set. My family is at the center. That's a bias with which I'm at peace. But I fail to see a clear moral line between human and non-human animals. I don't want to cause any sentient being to suffer or die. Of course, I fail at that too. I live in a suburb. I drive a car. I pay taxes. I buy fruits and vegetables from farms that use pesticides. I own an iPhone. I eat pepperoni pizza with our teenage daughters. There is no moral high ground. We all cause pain and suffering. All humans are hypocrites. All of us are complicit in the crimes of civilization.

Figure 5-6. A fuzzy moral circle.

Concurrently, we are beneficiaries of and contributors to the wonders of civilization. Backpacking in the wilderness offers a hint of what Thomas Hobbes called the state of nature: "continual fear and danger of violent death, and the life of man, solitary, poor, nasty, brutish, and short."[7] After a few days on Isle Royale, I was ready to kill for a hot shower and a flush toilet. It's easy to embrace *all good* or *all bad*, but we co-exist in the messy middle. We can't be perfect, but we can do better. While it's impractical to uphold the oath of Hippocrates to do no harm, it's certainly possible to do less harm. In no category of society is this more true than in medicine.

Iatrogenics is the third leading cause of death in the United States. Side effects, drug interactions, hospital infections, negligence, and surgical errors result in more than 225,000 deaths per year. The number of people who suffer each year from non-fatal, physician-induced illness runs into the millions. In *Hippocrates Shadow*, Dr. David Newman offers a powerful indictment of medical practice. Doctors routinely prescribe antibiotics for viral infections. This causes twenty-four thousand allergic reactions each year, not to mention several hundred thousand cases of diarrhea.[8] This is the tip of the iceberg. The scope and scale of iatrogenics is terrifying.

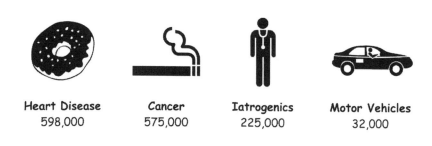

Heart Disease	Cancer	Iatrogenics	Motor Vehicles
598,000	575,000	225,000	32,000

Figure 5-7. Leading causes of death.

This does not mean all doctors are evil. Most of them believe they are doing good work. In fact, their confidence (and ours) is a large part of the problem. Our culture has an inordinate faith in the miracle of modern medicine, and a dangerous predisposition towards intervention. When we visit a physician, we expect diagnosis and prescription. We don't want our doctor to say "I don't know." But, more often than we know (or want to know), doctors truly don't know what they're doing. Our understanding of the complex systems that bind us together into billions of unique mixtures of mind-body-environment is limited. We're lost in the wilderness in the dark with a tiny flashlight. But we hate feeling helpless and want a quick fix, so we place our trust in the doctor.

We're not good at assigning trust. Bernie Madoff knew that well. We let what we want shift what we know. I do this all the time with the weather. I know the forecast isn't exact but want to ride my bike, so I try threading the needle between storms and end up soaked to the bone.

Sadly, our trust in doctors is even more misplaced, since malpractice isn't as random as a butterfly flapping its wings. With respect to our long-term health, a doctor doesn't have skin in the game. They don't suffer with us. To a degree, the opposite is true. Also, they are influenced by information and gifts delivered routinely by sales representatives of pharmaceutical and medical device companies. Again, they don't think this is wrong. Like journalists with advertisers or politicians with lobbyists, doctors tell themselves they're immune to influence. But we all know they are wrong.

Figure 5-8. The circle of trust.

Of course, even if doctors were solely motivated to help, the results might not be better, as their sources of information from research scientists to medical journals are also funded by pharma. If there's a serious health problem in our family, I consult Medline and the Cochrane Reviews, but even after hours of research, my confidence is low. In the United States, we spend $4 trillion a year on healthcare. The manufacture of consent is big business. It's hard to know who to trust.

That's why I've gone rogue. I haven't been to a doctor in years. I don't see my dentist either. If I have a serious problem, I'll consult a professional, but I believe checkups are dangerous. As Nassim Taleb says "If you want to accelerate someone's death, give him a personal doctor. I don't mean provide him with a bad doctor: just pay for him to choose his own. Any doctor will do."[9] Naïve intervention is a most deadly disease.

Our culture exaggerates the ability of doctors and drugs to improve our lives. We invest so much time and money in "health care," but it plays a minor role in health and longevity. That's why I pay more attention to my environment, economics, and behavior. I aim to change the things I can.

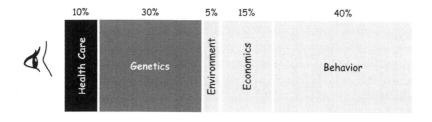

Figure 5-9. Effect upon health and longevity.

It's still hard to know what to do. Is skim milk in or out? Do we eat the bread, hold the butter, or vice versa? Simple questions about diet and exercise are surprisingly difficult to answer. I bumped into this realization a few years ago while trying to better my health. It all began with a Sunday morning ride on the Potawatomi trail. I was rolling down a hill when my front tire hit a root. My bike and I flipped end over end until the trail hit my back. Lucky to escape with bruised ribs, I decided trails were too risky, so I shifted my rides to roads. A few weeks later, I was hit by a car. It wasn't a bad accident. Only my bike was hurt. But it sure got my attention. I'd been enjoying my rides, but my overall goal was health. Is it safe to ride a bike? I needed to answer that question.

It took hours of searching, reading, and thinking to reach a conclusion. First, I had to figure out the politics. Cyclists and environmental groups have made "bike to work" into a movement. Cities around the country are building bike lanes and bike share systems. This is an exciting step towards a healthier society, but the interests of the individual and the community aren't always aligned. And the commitments to cycling that people and politicians have made has created a powerful, cultural bias. The media repeats "cycling is safe" like a mantra, but is this the truth, or is it the result of cultural self-justification and the manufacture of consent?

Popular articles were no good. I had to dig for statistics. I also realized I had to be realistic. Do you ride on trails, sidewalks, or streets? Do you live in Amsterdam or New York? Do you wear a helmet? How often do you drink, text and ride? No statistical sources isolate these variables, so there's no answer to my question. I set my sights lower, asking "Is it safe for me to train for triathlons by riding the roads of my community?"

The evidence suggests the answer is "No." In the United States, motor vehicle crashes are a leading cause of death. On a per trip basis, for adults age 25 to 64, riding a bike is four times more deadly.[10] By my calculations, each trip is relatively safe. I'm not afraid of riding to work on a whim. But if I routinely ride on the road for years, there's a good chance I'll be hit.

Figure 5-10. The probability of death per trip.

If I had to choose between road cycling and never cycling, I might take the risk, since I'm safer on a bike than on a couch. Low fitness is the single strongest predictor of death. Exercise lowers the risk of heart disease, diabetes, cancer, asthma, arthritis, anxiety, and the flu.[11] But I'm lucky to live in a town with a dedicated bike path. Now that's the only place I ride.

It began with a map and vision of a 35 mile border-to-border trail along the river. Today it's a reality that connects communities and protects people. Behavior is shaped by the context we create. What we build changes who we become. But we often don't know what to build. We're better at implementation than imagination. That's why we must use daylighting to design ourselves into a healthier future.

I'm still not safe. After my bike was hit, I told my mum. She knew this was my second mishap of the month and warned me to be careful as "these things come in threes." So I stayed off my bike. But weeks later while jogging I was savaged by a wiener dog. It bit a hole in my leg. You shouldn't be surprised. It's the most aggressive breed. One in five dachshunds bites a stranger. I now live in mortal fear of sausage dogs, but I doubt that's how I'll go. As I tell my wife whenever she's anxious, it's what you're not worrying about that will get you.

Understanding Limits

Our universe is 13.8 billion years old, so the diameter of the observable universe is 28 billion parsecs. The best way to grok this scale is through these words: "Space is big. Really big. You just won't believe how vastly hugely mind-bogglingly big it is. I mean, you may think it's a long way down the road to the chemist, but that's just peanuts to space."[12] Of course, Douglas Adams wrote that in 1979, and the universe is expanding at an ever increasing rate, so it's a lot bigger now.

In truth, we don't know the age or size of the universe. We have no idea what preceded the Big Bang. All we really know is that the answer is 42. But we're not about to let the universe get in the way of progress. We've developed all sorts of cognitive and cultural strategies to help us ignore our ignorance. Binary opposition and reductionism enable us to feel good about ourselves. We are good. They are bad. This is my area of expertise. That's not my problem. And most of the time this makes sense. We must feel safe to be useful. We must satisfice to survive. But, once in a while, we should embrace humility by reflecting upon the wisdom of Voltaire.

> Doubt is not a pleasant condition, but certainty is absurd.

When we question what we think we know, we engage in a philosophical inquiry with practical value. Certainty is the enemy of creativity. It blinds us to the possibility there might be a better way. Humility opens the door for collaboration. It invites us to ask questions and seek answers together.

In that spirit, *The Outer Limits of Reason* by Noson Yanofsky is a helpfully humbling study of the limitations of physics, logic, and our minds. A self-described *extreme nominalist*, the author explains his position as follows.

> Most people believe that there are certain objects in the universe and that human minds call those objects by names. What I am illustrating here is that those objects do not really exist. What do

exist are physical stimuli. Human beings classify and name those different stimuli as different objects.[13]

Yanofsky argues that we may learn more from looking at the way we are observing the universe than from the observation itself. To illustrate, he recalls a thought experiment of the philosopher-scientist Arthur Eddington.

> Suppose that an ichthyologist is exploring the life of the ocean. He casts a net into the water and brings up a fishy assortment. Surveying his catch, he proceeds in the usual manner of a scientist to systematize what it reveals. He arrives at two generalizations:
>
> 1) No sea-creature is less than two inches long.
>
> 2) All sea-creatures have gills. [14]

The catch stands for our scientific body of knowledge and the net for the sensory and cognitive apparatus used to obtain it. Together they invite a few questions. What's the relationship between catches and confidence? How many catches do we need? And how big are the holes in our net?

Figure 5-11. The limits of perception and cognition.

Of course, we often don't get what we do catch. For instance, Heisenberg's uncertainty principle tells us the position and momentum of a subatomic particle can't be measured concurrently with precision. This isn't a limit of technology but a consequence of the connectedness between observation and outcome. The properties of an object don't exist before they're measured. The experimenter is part of the experiment.

This leads to an even stranger aspect of quantum mechanics known as entanglement. In a pair of entangled particles, total spin is zero, so the instant one particle is measured and collapses into a spin direction, the other must collapse the opposite way, even if the two particles are light-years apart.

Einstein believed instant information transfer across infinite distance or "spooky action at a distance" to be impossible, but its effects have been shown experimentally. Researchers are exploring the use of entanglement for communication and computation. Recently, Dutch physicists were able to teleport quantum data over a ten foot distance with a replication rate of 100 percent.[15] It appears that Albert Einstein was wrong.

Figure 5-12. The consequence of quantum entanglement.

In his book, Yanofsky explains the philosophical consequences of the nonlocal effects of entanglement.

> One consequence of entanglement is to end the philosophical position of reductionism. This position says that if you want to understand some type of closed system, look at all the parts of the system. To understand how a radio works, one must take it apart and look at all its components, because "the whole is the sum of its

parts." Reductionism is a fundamental supposition in all of science. Entanglement shows that there are no closed systems.[16]

All systems are interconnected. This subatomic truth resonates equally at global scale. It's this vital insight that motivates people to care for the health of their environment, and it's the first of Barry Commoner's four laws of ecology.[17]

1. Everything is connected to everything else.

2. Everything must go somewhere.

3. Nature knows best.

4. There is no such thing as a free lunch.

Interdependence is also the basis of systems thinking. It explains why the whole is more than the sum of its parts and why our ability to predict or control the behavior of complex adaptive systems is less than we think. In 1972, Donella Meadows and her colleagues at MIT explained the potential consequences of interactions between natural and human systems in their landmark book, *The Limits to Growth*.[18] They used a computer model with five major variables – world population, industrialization, pollution, food production, resource depletion – to explore a range of possible scenarios.

They saw that if growth trends remained unchanged, we'd experience a sudden, uncontrollable decline in population and industrial capacity within the next hundred years. This scary conclusion garnered worldwide attention. The book sold more than 12 million copies in 37 languages and helped launch the environmental movement. But it was also widely criticized as a Malthusian doomsday prophecy that failed to recognize the enormous power of technology, democracy, and capitalism.

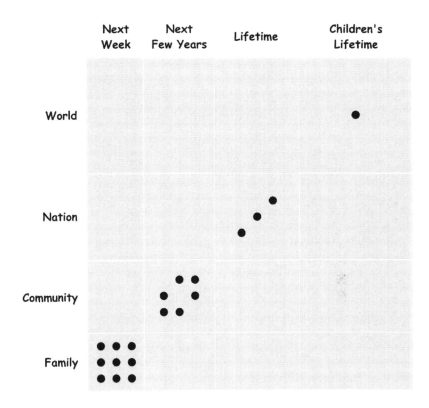

Figure 5-13. The limits of human perspective.

Donella realized change would not be easy, since our actions are centered on issues that affect our friends and family in the near term. However, she felt a tremendous sense of urgency, because she understood that if we waited until the limits were obvious, it would be too late to avoid an overshoot.

The three causes of overshoot are always the same, at any scale from personal to planetary. First, there is growth, acceleration, rapid change. Second, there is some form of limit or barrier, beyond which the moving system may not safely go. Third, there is a delay or mistake in the perceptions and the responses that strive to keep the system within its limits.[19]

She expected attacks from those with financial and political interests in growth, and she knew they'd appeal to our deep cultural faith in markets and technology.

Markets and technologies are merely tools that serve the goals, the ethics, and the time horizons of the society as a whole. If a society's implicit goals are to exploit nature, enrich the elites, and ignore the long term, then that society will develop technologies and markets that destroy the environment, widen the gap between the rich and the poor, and optimize for short term gains.[20]

In fact, she noted that "technological optimism is the most common and the most dangerous reaction to our findings" since "technology can relieve the symptoms of a problem without affecting the underlying causes."[21]

Despite her willingness to confront reality and speak truth to power, Donella was an optimist, arguing "it is possible to alter these growth trends and to establish a condition of ecological and economic stability that is sustainable far into the future."

Sadly, while her book made an impact, it has not yet meaningfully altered the trajectory of humanity. Today, we are in ecological overshoot. Both global population and per capita resource use continue to grow. It now takes the Earth a year and six months to regenerate what we use in a year.

Climate change is the most notorious impact, but there are many less visible consequences. For instance, we are responsible for the loss of biodiversity on a massive scale. In *The Sixth Extinction*, Elizabeth Kolbert catalogs the destruction.

Today, amphibians enjoy the dubious distinction of being the world's most endangered class of animals; it's been calculated that the group's extinction rate could be as much as forty-five thousand times higher than the background rate. But extinction rates among many other groups are approaching amphibian levels. It is estimated that one-third of all reef-building corals, a third of all freshwater mollusks, a third of sharks and rays, a quarter of all mammals, a fifth of all reptiles, and a sixth of all birds are headed toward oblivion.[22]

Much of this damage is due to increased carbon dioxide in the atmosphere and oceans, but our travel and shipping also have unintended consequences. Thanks to hitchhikers on our boats and planes, Hawaii acquires one invasive species a month. Before humans settled the islands, this occurred once every 10,000 years. We are the agents of chaos. As Elizabeth Kolbert says "those of us alive today not only are witnessing one of the rarest events in life's history, we are also causing it."[23]

So how does this story end? We have no idea. We may not change course. As Jared Diamond illustrated in *Collapse*, "societies often fail even to attempt to solve a problem once it has been perceived."[24] But Donella Meadows never gave up. She believed in people and the power of information.

> Information is the key to transformation. That does not necessarily mean more information, better statistics, bigger databases, or the World Wide Web, though all of these may play a part. It means relevant, compelling, select, powerful, timely, accurate information flowing in new ways to new recipients, carrying new content, suggesting new rules and goals (that are themselves information). When its information flows are changed, any system will behave differently.[25]

Of course as Calvin Mooers warned, information has its limits.

> Many people may not want information, and they will avoid using a system precisely because it gives them information. Having information is painful and troublesome. We have all experienced this. If you have information, you must first read it, which is not always easy. You must then try to understand it. Understanding the information may show that your work was wrong, or may show that your work was needless. Thus not having and not using information can often lead to less trouble and pain.[26]

It's been 42 years since *The Limits to Growth* hit us hard. The book put a dent in the universe. But it hasn't changed our trajectory. Nobody knows how to stop humanity from sawing off the limb on which we stand. But one thing is sure. If we rely on information alone to bridge the gap between understanding and action, we'd better be ready to swim. People fail to act on information all the time. We know soda is a toxic substance, but we drink it anyway. We know quarterly earnings is a terrible metric that threatens the long-term health of a business, but we use it anyway.

Information is not enough. We should map the hidden pathways of our natural and organizational ecosystems, but then we must act. At multiple levels, as individuals, organizations, and societies, we must embrace divergent ways of changing what we want and what we do. An awareness of the entangled nature of systems is essential, but it's equally vital to have the right attitude. There are moments in a marathon when we can't see our way to the goal. We know we'll soon hit the wall. We've lost faith. But we still have hope. So we keep on running. Eventually we will find a way.

Interbeing

The number of humans living on Earth is mind-bogglingly big. It's not infinite like the universe, but it's big enough to make us feel small. Mostly we ignore this larger context. Our habits and culture help us to focus on the task at hand. But, once in a while, we ask big questions. Why am I here? Where (and when) am I going? What's the something only I can do?

In my personal life, I try to be a good dad, husband, brother, son, and friend. I do this in part by caring for my health, since it's vital to "secure your own mask before helping others." In my professional life, I aim to be a good information architect. I do this by mixing consulting, speaking, and writing. I relish the challenge of a new organizational ecosystem, and I love wrangling with strategy and structure to find the right fit. But I'm also driven to consider this work in its next larger context.

What are the relationships between categories, connections, and culture? Where are the links, loops, and levers? How can we use our ways of seeing to effect change at a higher level? I speak and write so we might understand and act together. We know what we think when we see what we say.

Of course, our personal and professional lives are wholly intertwingled. Compartmentalism is a dangerous myth. We can't be callous at work and loving at home. The centre cannot hold. The wall will not stand. How we do anything is how we do everything. We know this but it's hard to put into practice. Our culture stuffs everything inside little boxes except for all those externalities that don't exist. Our vision is further narrowed by information anxiety which tricks us into fight or flight. Neither option is healthy. The path to peace begins with awareness of what Thich Nhat Hanh calls "interbeing."

If you are a poet, you will see clearly that there is a cloud floating in this sheet of paper. Without a cloud, there will be no rain; without rain, the trees cannot grow; and without trees, we cannot make paper. The cloud is essential for the paper to exist. If the cloud is not here, the sheet of paper cannot be here either.[27]

Hanh uses interbeing to remind us that to be is to inter-be. Everything's linked. We can't isolate our selves from context.

A mother holding her baby is one with her baby.

If it does not grow well, you don't blame the lettuce.

It's hard to hold these truths to be self-evident in a ship of state that's listing dangerously from democracy to capitalism to oligarchy. Ben Franklin stated in 1776 that "we must all hang together, or assuredly we shall all hang separately," but what our culture says today is "every man for himself."

For a moment, the Internet was our hope. We thought we were building an information commons, a shared peer-to-peer network created by and accessible to all. But this place made of information became subject to the process of enclosure. Like our fields and forests and universities and hospitals, it was corporatized and commodified. Donella Meadows was right about technology. In the long run, it reflects and reinforces the dominant culture. No tail can wag the dog for long.

In contrast, the free public library has managed to endure. It's a source of information and inspiration that tells a tale of rags to riches, not the rich get richer. Andrew Carnegie nailed it back in 1889 when he explained "a library outranks any other one thing a community can do to benefit its people. It is a never failing spring in the desert." The library is one of the last surviving places where we are citizens, not consumers. When we ask a librarian for trusted counsel, their only motives are to teach us to search and to help us to find what we need. And the library is a treasure for the independent learner. It may still be the only place where a dirt poor kid like Andrew Carnegie can access databases, the Internet, and books.

Of course, the library isn't only a space for information. Public libraries share all sorts of things, including tools, toys, and telescopes. And they afford a peaceful refuge where an individual can escape to read, write, search, think, and learn. A library, like a national park, teaches us that we all benefit when our most valuable treasures are held in common.

Figure 5-14. Libraries share more than books.

In a society with rising inequality, libraries aim to level the playing field. There's substance to this mission, but its role is symbolic too. Like public schools and parks, libraries remind us that capitalism-socialism is a false dichotomy. The path to health starts with synthesis, but we're held hostage by this sickness of binary opposition. From whence does either-or dualism come, and why are we unable to break its spell? The answer may lie in myths, our stories of culture used to teach morals to kids. Consider, for instance, *The Ant and Grasshopper*.

> In a field one summer's day a Grasshopper was hopping about, chirping and singing to its heart's content. An Ant passed by, bearing along with great toil an ear of corn he was taking to the nest. "Why not come and chat with me," said the Grasshopper, "instead of toiling and moiling in that way?"

"I am helping to lay up food for the winter," said the Ant, "and recommend you to do the same."

"Why bother about winter?" said the Grasshopper. "We have got plenty of food at present." But the Ant went on its way and continued its toil. When the winter came the Grasshopper had no food and found itself dying of hunger, while it saw the ants distributing every day corn and grain from the stores they had collected in the summer. Then the Grasshopper knew: it is best to prepare for the days of necessity.

On the surface, it's a simple tale about two animals that offers children a lesson in common sense. But morals work like maps by hiding more than they reveal. Aesop paints in black and white. His story leaves no room for the grasshopper, which is precisely the point of an opposite fable by Daniel Quinn about a telepathic gorilla and his human student with an earnest desire to save the world. *Ishmael* is a story of Leavers and Takers. Leavers are herders and hunter-gatherers who leave fate in the hands of the gods. Takers are agriculturalists and technologists who take the law of nature into their own hands. Takers are the people of our culture who believe man is the center of the universe, there is one right way to live, and there are no limits to growth. Leavers are the peoples of all ancient cultures who lived in harmony with their environments for millions of years until the Takers made them nearly extinct.

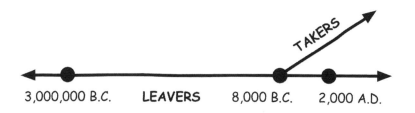

Figure 5-15. Timeline of Leavers and Takers.

Ishmael explains to his student that in the tumultuous period since Takers emerged roughly ten thousand years ago, they have ruthlessly, relentlessly destroyed diversity.

> The knowledge of what works well for people is what's valued in Leaver cultures. And every time the Takers stamp out a Leaver culture, a wisdom ultimately tested since the birth of mankind disappears from the world beyond recall, just as every time they stamp out a species of life, a life form ultimately tested since the birth of life disappears from the world beyond recall.[28]

It's a powerful indictment of our civilization and the saddest story I've ever read. In *Ishmael*, the Grasshopper lives in peace with nature, the Ant is hell-bent on consuming the world, and that's the trouble I have with both myths. The classification of people into two categories is part of the problem. Fables reflect and reinforce our innate bias for binary opposition. They encourage us to ostracize them. But if we realize what's going on, and the danger of dichotomy is gone, then we can explore new ways of seeing stories. For instance, the tortoise and the hare aren't two kinds of people but opposite ends of a strategic spectrum. We each have the capacity to sprint or plod, and there's not only one way to win. Similarly, each of us can be a fox who knows many things or a hedgehog who knows one big thing. The best strategy depends on context.

Once our eyes are open, myths can be paths to wisdom. They help us understand ourselves and our culture. Consider, for instance, the cross-cultural archetype of the *trickster*, a subversive character who is often both hero and buffoon. Anansi, Brer Rabbit, Coyote, Loki, Raven: the trickster is a shapeshifter, a familiar outsider who transgresses boundaries in the folklore of many cultures. A creature of ambiguity and liminality, the trickster breaks rules, plays games, defies categories, and upsets the dominant order. He may be wise, foolish, noble, and mean. He's a deeply entangled paradox.

Of course, the trickster isn't a myth. He's real. He lives in Silicon Valley. He has a gift for you. It's a wearable computer with a heads-up display or a cloud-based home security solution or a drone that delivers pizza or a toilet that monitors your health. It's easy to use. It just works. And you know what's insanely great? It's free. So give us your eyeballs now.

When I was a kid in England, I rode a yellow skateboard. I learned to fall and to ollie and that the future is invented in California. Over time I've been a loyal consumer. I've bought Apple computers, HP printers, and Cisco routers. I've also been a producer with clients in Cupertino, Mountain View, Palo Alto, San José, San Francisco, and Sunnyvale. I'm great friends with the Valley. It's a wonderful place to be.

Tricksters are exasperating because they're so good and bad at once. The iPhone isn't simply useful, usable, and desirable. It's a work of art. But it's also an ugly status symbol, a driving distraction, and an environmental nightmare. Fitbit, Jawbone, and Pebble are fascinating fitness tracking devices, but do we even know whether they're making us more healthy or less?

I'm not sure how to manage this trickster, but I do know we must shift from self-justification to self-awareness to move ahead. The secular myth of disruptive innovation isn't new, but it is effective. We're so busy searching for dinosaurs, we forget to look where we're going. In 2004 when Bruce Sterling first spoke of spime – speculative objects precisely located in space and time – the vision he painted was bright green. Transfigured from passive consumers into heroic wranglers, we would mash products, sensors, RFID, and GPS into *sustainable spime* to reduce, reuse, and recycle like never before.

> It's possible to live in a cleaner way. We live in debris and detritus because of our ignorance. That ignorance is no longer technically necessary…Our capacities are tremendous. Eventually, it is within our technical ability to create factories that clean the air as they work, cars that give off drinkable water, industry that creates parks instead of dumps, or even monitoring systems that allow nature to thrive in our cities, neighborhoods, lawns and homes. An industry that is not just "sustainable," but enhances the world.[29]

A decade later, not only are we not there yet, but we may be traveling in the opposite direction. Are the espoused values of tricksters clouding our vision? What are the real assumptions, beliefs, and values of Silicon Valley? What is the theory of the world behind self-driving cars, wearable devices, ingestible sensors, clones, drones, and the Singularity? Of course, we shouldn't be too hard on the technologists, since we won't even have a future unless we invent ourselves out of the box.

The root of our problem is on the opposite coast. Our federal government is corrupt and riddled with tricksters who are neither wise nor noble. Until we rid ourselves of this pollution, and unless we learn to design systems of governance that can't be corrupted by those who score high on the sociopath scale, we will not find the way. Our daughter surprised us a few years back by stating as a matter of fact "Of course civilization will collapse soon. I only hope it doesn't happen while I'm still around." Is this the legacy we bequeath to our children, or can we imagine and invent a world of better tomorrows?

Liminality is the quality of ambiguity or disorientation that occurs during periods of transition. It's the ugly duckling stage of life, the "in between" in a rite of passage, and the barely perceptible threshold in a change of mind. At a societal level, the dissolution of order and the loss of traditions and institutions during liminal times make us vulnerable to the trickster. In the hunt for a charismatic leader to save us, it's easy to lose ourselves. We must be vigilant. We must nurture self-awareness while seeking answers outside our model of the system. We shouldn't rush, but there isn't much time. We can't keep up the pace. Our energy use is unsustainable. Our capacity for change has limits. This era will end. Our ways of being and believing will shift. Liminality is not the goal.

It's time to reveal the hero of our story is not the trickster but the tree. A clever mind delivers a quick fix, but the road to eternity is a garden of branching paths. We've been living in relationship with trees since time immemorial. Trees are invaluable sources of food, shelter, medicine, tools, fire, and wisdom. In ancient myth, the roots, trunk, and canopy of the *World Tree* connected the earth to the heavens and the underworld. In Buddhist legend, the Buddha achieved enlightenment under the heart-shaped leaves of the *Bodhi Tree*. Adam and Eve were banished from the *Tree of Life* after being tricked into eating from the *Tree of Knowledge of Good and Evil*. As Thich Nhat Hanh tells us, trees are part of our perception. When we read "I am the Lorax. I speak for the trees," our minds mingle with the ideas and words of the author in a cloud or on a sheet of paper. Trees are ancient symbols in our collective unconscious. The tree is the archetype of interbeing.

All my life, animals have wandered into my world. When we lived in England, we had a tiny backyard surrounded by a wooden fence. One Sunday, I watched a tortoise walk under the gate and into our garden. We adopted him. My sister named him Batman. We also discovered a hedgehog who chose to hibernate in the wardrobe where we kept our tools. My brother named him King Henry VIII. For a time, we believed our milkman was a thief, until we saw the crows stealing our milk. And in Michigan, in recent years, a fox family moved in next door. My wife, our daughters, and I love to watch the mama and her spirited children play in the grass in the Spring. These animals are symbols of freedom. They walk into our lives and remind us our boundaries don't exist.

The story of man versus nature makes no sense. The relationship is hierarchical. Man is part of nature, and so is all that we build. No system is closed. Externalities are delusions. There is no free lunch. These truths resonate on all levels for individuals, organizations, and societies. If we hope to get better, we must respect the nature of information in systems and nurture the health of the whole. This is not only a technical challenge. We must shift culture too. It won't be easy. The system always kicks back. But it's not impossible.

Figure 5-16. Nature is the root directory.

By exposing our categories and connections to the light of day, we become responsible for the consequences of our actions. As a wise woman once said, it can happen in the blink of an eye.

> It can happen in a millisecond. All it takes is a click in the mind, a falling of scales from eyes, a new way of seeing.

To get better at getting better, we must see there are no limits. Our models are all we know. We draw edges that don't exist. This isn't bad but dangerous, and it makes us uncomfortable. That's okay. We must learn to sit with our discomfort. Instead of burying guilt and fear in little boxes, we must admit black swans and externalities into our model of the system, because information changes everything. If we allow ourselves to be aware of connectedness, to see everything is intertwingled, and to act on the reality of interbeing, then we will hopefully change what we want, and that is the path we must travel.

Notes

Chapter 1

[1] The Wolves and Moose of Isle Royale by John Vucetich (2011).

[2] An ice bridge formed this past winter, the first since 2008, and lasted 16 days. Researchers didn't observe any newcomers, but for the first time did document wolf traffic in the opposite direction. One of the radio-collared adults lost from Isle Royale, a lone female nicknamed Isabelle, was found dead on the northeastern Minnesota shore. An autopsy later revealed the cause of death: a pellet gunshot in the chest.

[3] Pervasive Information Architecture by Andrea Resmini and Luca Rosati (2011).

[4] Architectures by Jorge Arango (2011).

[5] Understanding Context by Andrew Hinton (2014).

[6] Make Things Be Good by Dan Klyn (2013).

[7] Systemantics by John Gall (1975), p.14.

[8] Systems Thinking for Curious Managers by Russell Ackoff (2010), p.6.

[9] Thinking in Systems by Donella Meadows (2008), p.14.

[10] Meadows (2008), p.157.

[11] Meadows (2008), p.5.

[12] The Death and Life of Great American Cities by Jane Jacobs (1961), p.376.

[13] Jacobs (1961), p.376.

[14] The Agile Manifesto, http://agilemanifesto.org.

[15] The Machine That Changed the World by James Womack (1990), p.56.

[16] The Lean Startup by Eric Ries (2011).

[17] Meadows (2008), p.170.

[18] Should Isle Royale Wolves Be Reintroduced by John Vucetich (2012), p.130.

[19] The Perfect Mile by Neal Bascomb (2005).

Chapter 2

[1] Philosophy of the Buddha by Christopher W. Gowans (2003), p.29.

[2] Mindfulness in Plain English by Bhante Gunaratana (2011), p.151.

[3] Gunaratana (2011), p.168.

[4] Why Americans are the Weirdest People in the World by Ethan Watters (2013).

[5] The Concept of Mind by Gilbert Ryle (1949), p.5.

[6] Supersizing the Mind by Andy Clark (2011), p.xxviii.

[7] The Extended Mind by Andy Clark and David J. Chalmers (1998).

[8] The Crayola-Fication of the World by Aatish Bhatia (2012).

[9] Basic Color Terms by Brent Berlin and Paul Kay (1969).

[10] Hippocrates' Shadow by David H. Newman (2008), p.12.

[11] Drug Companies and Doctors: A Story of Corruption by Marcia Angell (2009).

[12] Thinking in Systems by Donella Meadows (2008), p.174.

[13] Soldiers sometimes use Silly String to detect tripwires without detonating the explosives.

[14] Sorting Things Out: Classification and its Consequences by Geoffrey C. Bowker and Susan Leigh Star (1999), p.5.

[15] Why Dewey's Decimal System is Prejudiced by David Weinberger (2004).

[16] Gowans (2003), p.41.

[17] Women, Fire, and Dangerous Things by George Lakoff (1987), p.13.

[18] How Netflix Reverse Engineered Hollywood by Alexis C. Madrigal (2014).

[19] Lakoff (1987), p.271.

[20] Fundamentals of Language by Roman Jakobson and Morris Halle (1956), p.60.

[21] Semiotics: The Basics by Daniel Chandler (2002), p.111.

[22] Conversion, Culture, and Cognitive Categories by Paul G. Hiebert (1978).

[23] Centered and Bounded Sets by Dan Klyn (2012).

[24] Life of Pi by Yann Martel (2003), p.66.

[25] To learn more about holacracy, see holacracy.org.

[26] The Death and Life of Great American Cities by Jane Jacobs (1961), p.392.

[27] The New Library Patron by Lee Rainie (2013).

[28] The Timeless Way of Building by Christopher Alexander (1979).

[29] The Battle for the Life and Beauty of the Earth by Christopher Alexander, Hans Joachim Neis, and Maggie Moore Alexander (2012), p.115.

[30] Information Anxiety by Richard Saul Wurman (1989), p.72.

[31] The Wurmanizer by Gary Wolf (2000).

[32] Dutch Uncles, Ducks, and Decorated Sheds by Dan Klyn (2013).

[33] A Brief History of Information Architecture by Andrea Resmini and Luca Rosati (2012).

[34] Wurman (1989), p.59.

[35] The Clock of the Long Now by Stewart Brand (1999), p.34.

[36] How Buildings Learn by Stewart Brand (1995).

[37] Resilience: Why Things Bounce Back by Andrew Zolli (2013), p.34.

[38] Don't Just Be the Change: Mass-Produce It by Alex Steffen (2007).

[39] Why Dolphins Make Us Nervous by Robert Krulwich (2013).

[40] Nonhuman Rights Project, http://www.nonhumanrights.org.

[41] Your Body Is Younger Than You Think by Nicholas Wade.

[42] What is the Function of the Claustrum? by Francis Crick, Christof Koch (2005).

[43] A "black swan" is a pivotal event that's hard to predict or imagine in advance. Nassim Taleb popularized the term in his book, The Black Swan (2007).

Chapter 3

[1] Soon Love Soon by Vienna Teng, https://archive.org/details/VTatWaterHill.

[2] Cataloging the World by Alex Wright (2014).

[3] As We May Think by Vannevar Bush (1945).

[4] Project Xanadu by Ted Nelson, http://www.xanadu.com.

[5] A Research Center for Augmenting Human Intellect by Doug Englebart (1968).

[6] Englebart's violin was a chorded keyboard designed to be used in concert with a traditional typewriter keyboard and a mouse.

[7] The Design of Browsing and Berrypicking Techniques by Marcia J. Bates (1989).

[8] Information Foraging by Peter Pirolli and Stuart Card (1995).

[9] Service Design by Andy Polaine, Lavrans Lovlie, and Ben Reason (2013), p.86.

[10] On the Drucker Legacy by Robert Klitgaard (2006).

[11] The Black Swan by Nicholas Nassim Taleb (2007), p.40.

[12] On Intelligence by Jeff Hawkins (2004), p.87.

[13] The Tell-Tale Brain by V. S. Ramachandran (2011), p.55.

[14] Hawkins (2004), p.89.

[15] Teaching Smart People How to Learn by Chris Argyris (1991).

[16] Models of My Life by Herbert Simon (1991), p.xvii.

[17] Making Sense of the Organization by Karl Weick (2001), p.195.

[18] Weick (2001), p.369.

[19] Stop Worrying About Making the Right Decision by Ed Batista (2013).

[20] Mistakes Were Made (But Not By Me) by Carol Tavris et al. (2007), p.32.

[21] Weick (2001), p.27.

[22] Gamestorming by Dave Gray, Sunni Brown, and James Macanufo (2010).

[23] Antifragile: Things That Gain from Disorder by Nassim Nicholas Taleb (2012).

[24] Weick (2001), p.371.

[25] The Cathedral and the Bazaar by Eric Raymond (1999), p.73.

[26] What is the Theory of Your Firm? by Todd Zenger (2013).

[27] The Back of the Napkin by Dan Roam (2008), p.120.

[28] What is Strategy? by Michael Porter (1996).

[29] Ramachandran (2011), p.xiv.

[30] Ramachandran (2011), p.105.

Chapter 4

[1] The Corporate Culture Survival Guide by Edgar Schein (1999), p.27.

[2] Schein (1999), p.5.

[3] Cultures and Organizations by Geert Hofstede et al. (2010), p.8.

[4] Hofstede (2010), p.9.

[5] Hofstede (2010), p.20.

[6] Technology and Social Interaction by Brigitte Jordan (1992).

[7] The Interpretation of Cultures by Clifford Geertz (1973), p.5.

[8] Geertz (1973), p.6.

[9] The Ethnographic Interview by James Spradley (1979), p.17.

[10] Spradley (1979), p.34.

[11] Spradley (1979), p.19.

[12] Spradley (1979), p.18.

[13] Hofstede (2010), p.350.

[14] Schein (1999), p.58.

[15] Spradley (1979), p.93.

[16] Spradley (1979), adapted from Figure 5.1, p.102.

[17] Spradley (1979), adapted from Figure 10.1, p.176.

[18] The Fifth Discipline by Peter Senge (1990), p.57.

[19] Senge (1990), p.88.

[20] Senge (1990), p.63.

[21] Schein (1999), p.34.

[22] Schein (1999), p.223.

[23] Schein (1999), p.86.

[24] Leading from the Emerging Future by Otto Scharmer and Katrim Kaufer (2013), p.16.

[25] Nudge by Richard Thaler and Cass Sunstein (2008), p.3.

[26] Thaler and Sunstein (2008), p.1.

[27] Thaler and Sunstein (2008), p.71.

[28] Thaler and Sunstein (2008), p.111.

[29] Culture Mapping by Dave Gray.

[30] The Power of Habit by Charles Duhigg (2012), p.139.

[31] The Fastest Way to Make Change (2012).

[32] Meetup's Dead Simple User Testing (2008).

[33] Duhigg (2012), p.98.

[34] Duhigg (2012), p.116.

[35] The Folkways Collection, Episode 12: Pete Seeger.

[36] Managing Emergence by Marc Rettig (2014).

[37] The Power of Positive Deviance by David Marsh et al. (2004).

[38] The Tell Tale Brain by V.S. Ramachandran (2011), p.117.

[39] The Long-Term Impact of IT Culture by Brenda Laurel (1997).

Chapter 5

[1] Run Less, Run Faster by Bill Pierce, Scott Murr, and Ray Moss (2007).

[2] Strategy Safari by Henry Mintzberg, Bruce Ahlstrand, Joseph Lampel (1998), p. 373.

[3] Strategy and Structure by Alfred Chandler (1962).

[4] Strategy and Structure by Alfred Chandler (1990).

[5] Scenarios: Shooting the Rapids by Pierre Wack (1985).

[6] Daylighting Streams: Breathing Life into Urban Streams and Communities.

[7] Leviathan by Thomas Hobbes (1651).

[8] Hippocrates Shadow by David Newman (2008), p.30.

[9] Antifragile by Nassim Nicholas Taleb (2012), p.125.

[10] Motor Vehicle Crash Injury Rates by Mode of Travel (2007).

[11] The Exercise Cure by Dr. Jordan Metzl (2013).

[12] The Hitchhiker's Guide to the Galaxy by Douglas Adams (1979), p.76.

[13] The Outer Limits of Reason by Noson Yanofsky (2013), p.40.

[14] Yanofsky (2013), p.291.

[15] Scientists Report Finding Reliable Way to Teleport Data by John Markoff (2014).

[16] Yanofsky (2013), p.201.

[17] The Closing Circle by Barry Commoner (1971).

[18] The Limits to Growth by Donella Meadows, Dennis Meadows, Jorgen Randers, and William Behrens III (1972).

[19] Meadows (1972), p.1.

[20] Beyond the Limits by Donella Meadows, Dennis Meadows, and Jorgen Randers (1992).

[21] Meadows (1972), p.154.

[22] The Sixth Extinction by Elizabeth Kolbert (2014), p.17.

[23] Kolbert (2014), p.7.

[24] Collapse by Jared Diamond (2005), p.427.

[25] The Limits to Growth by Donella Meadows et al. (2004), p.269.

[26] Remarks by Calvin N. Mooers on October 24, 1959. Reprinted in the Bulletin of the American Society for Information Science, October/November 1996.

[27] Peace is Every Step by Thich Nhat Hanh (1991), p.95.

[28] Ishmael by Daniel Quinn (1992), p.206.

[29] Bruce Sterling, When Blobjects Rule the Earth (2004).

Index

structure, 7, 19, 107, 145
subcultures, 115–21
synesthesia, 107
synthesis, 16, 28, 138, 169
Systemantics, 13
systems thinking, 11–22

T

tagging, 61
Taleb, Nassim, 93, 102, 156
taxonomy, 33, 40, 47, 50, 55, 129
technological optimism, 164
Teng, Vienna, 80
Tetris, 42
thick description, 129
Thinking in Systems, 16
tiny habits, 134
tortoise, 171, 174
Toyota, 25
tranquility, 77–79
translation competence, 125
transparent equipment, 41
trees, 174
tribalism, 66
tricksters, 171
trust, 12, 21, 31, 45, 50, 52, 123,
    155, 168

U

Uber, 11
uncomfortable, viii, 6, 11, 29, 175
understanding limits, 159–66
unintended consequences, 91, 97, 165

University of Michigan, 6, 110
urban planning, 19
user experience, 8, 32, 64, 67, 112,
    147, 149

V

vipassanā, 39
volleyball, 109, 143

W

Wack, Pierre, 146
Walden Pond, 36
water filtration system, 26
Water Hill Music Festival, 80
ways of knowing, 121–24
Weick, Karl, 88, 101, 103
Whitman, Walt, 38
Winchester Mystery House, 22
wireframes, 7, 103
wisdom, 94, 100, 123, 171
Wittgenstein, Ludwig, 66
Wurman, Richard Saul, 9, 73, 87

X

Xanadu, 81, 108

Y

Yanofsky, Noson, 159
yathā bhūta, 79
yin-yang, 70
yoga, 47

About the Author

Peter Morville is a widely respected pioneer of the fields of information architecture and user experience. His best-selling books include *Information Architecture for the World Wide Web* (also known as "the bible of IA" and "the polar bear book"), *Ambient Findability*, and *Search Patterns*. He advises such clients as AT&T, Cisco, Harvard, IBM, the Library of Congress, and the National Cancer Institute. He has delivered conference keynotes and workshops in North America, South America, Europe, Asia, and Australia. His work has been covered by *Business Week*, *The Economist*, *NPR*, and *The Wall Street Journal*.

Peter lives in Ann Arbor, Michigan with his wife, two lovely daughters, and a dog named Knowsy. When he's not running, biking, swimming, or hiking, you can find him on the Internet at *semanticstudios.com* and *intertwingled.org*.

15917874R00113

Made in the USA
San Bernardino, CA
11 October 2014